# A Sense of Joy

*Words of encouragement and inspiration
from a psychotherapist*

## Peter Field

red valley
PUBLISHING

Field, Peter
A Sense of Joy
   1. Psychology
   I. Title
ISBN 978-1-909257-20-7

innerhealing@email.com

http://www.peterfieldhypnotherapy.co.uk

In memory of my brother
Bob Field

# Contents

# Foreword

~

I n the introduction to this book, Peter Field suggests that his work be read slowly, so that his readers may be allowed to incubate these writings and give birth to an emerging deep understanding of *A Sense of Joy*.

In his work as a therapist, the writer notes that he 'takes others by the hand and walks by their side.' He observes that we may remain stationary for long periods on our life's journey, fearing closed doors and windows that act as mirrors. By showing us a way to do so through his sensitive prose, he assists us on our own unique journeys. He encourages us to open metaphorical doors so that we may transcend our fear of them and the brutal surprises we expect to be behind them. He asks us to distill the images of self-reflection that we see in our metaphorical mirrors, so that we can perceive ourselves as we are, without contortion and distortion of ourselves.

In terms of his observation of the world, Peter does not dismiss reality as being devoid of suffering. Instead, he looks bravely at the world's inhumanity and destructiveness, such as that confronting him when he visited Auschwitz. He then juxtaposes the brutality of the world with his perception of meaning, stating that there is 'more to be loved than hated' in the world. Paradoxically, he conceives out of life's cruelty a response of love and joy, which he shares through the thoughtful emotional rhythm of his prose.

*A Sense of Joy* conveys a ruminative and gentle demonstration of kindness toward humanity that the author has offered to those who are fortunate in discovering this book. In reading this work, one will realise that the writing ensues from a love of others, and that the healing involved in the message of the book belongs not only to those who follow his words and meditations, but to anyone who is ready to receive the love that Peter sees and reveals in life and expresses as a gift to his readers.

**Dr Ann Reitan, Doctor of Psychology**

*Fresno, California*

# Preface

~

$F$ ew people have the gift of articulating the human experience in words quite like Peter Field. *A Sense of Joy* is filled with valuable insights and recommendations on how to live a life that is full of meaning and joy.

We all strive to find balance in life, to experience true happiness and contentment. As a psychotherapist, Peter has had the opportunity to observe first hand the one thing that seems to hold so many of us back from achieving our hearts desires: Ourselves. In this collection of meditations, you will learn that you and you alone hold the keys to unlocking your true self and overcoming obstacles.

Getting 'unstuck' from the mire of failures, insecurities, and anxieties can be difficult, but it is not impossible. The good news is that we all have the ability to get unstuck by taking action *right now*, not tomorrow or next week or after we have achieved a specific goal. Every single day we have a new opportunity to *choose* to make a positive change. That, in and of itself, is powerful. Acknowledging you have this ability is your first step towards a renewed self. In Peter's words, '...the smallest action has much more power than even the best thought out intention.'

The fact that you have chosen to read Peter's book means that you are ready to change... and you've taken your first step.

One of my favorite quotes is by George Eliot, 'It's never too late to be what you might have been.' Reinventing ourselves is one of the most awesome gifts we have. You can read and talk and contemplate on what you want in life, but unless you take action, nothing will change.

3

As you read this book notice how Peter consistently reminds us that we have the power to choose how we respond to life. In every situation, with every thought, in every moment, in every breath, we have a choice.

In reading this book, you will find a friend in Peter. His words are poignant, comforting and insightful. You cannot read his words and not be changed. I think one of my favorite phrases he writes is, 'Today your life begins all over again.' I would encourage you to sit quietly, close your eyes and meditate on this concept. Then do something about it. Do this every day and you will revolutionise the way you live your life.

**Dr Kathy Seigler**
*Clinical Psychologist*

# Introduction

~

The idea for this book did not come from me, but from a close friend who asked why I didn't make my columns available in printed form. 'Why consign them to the nether reaches of cyberspace?' he said, 'I know you're taking them off your website in order to make more room, but it would be nice to have some of them in my pocket. And I'm sure I'm not the only one who'd like that'.

Would it be nice? The simple answer was that I hadn't really thought of it, something not at all surprising, since there is an awful lot that I have never thought of.

A couple of years ago, that wonderful American therapist the late Gil Boyne sent me a very warm email telling me how much he had been moved by one of my columns. I think it was *An Attitude of Gratitude*, the column I wrote after my return from Auschwitz. 'My wife has printed it out and has it in her purse', he said.

But still the penny didn't drop. I just kept on writing the columns and putting them online, hoping they might interest and, perhaps in some small way, help other people.

None of these pages were really written to go into a book. I wrote them as monthly columns for my hypno-psychotherapy website, and I have to admit that some were dashed off in order to meet deadlines, but I like to think that every one was written from the heart, with maybe just a little help from the head. I've tweaked them a little, just to nudge them into a weekly, rather than the original monthly format, but apart from that they remain the same.

Perhaps I wrote them in an attempt to bring a degree of comfort and joy to those who were finding life a bit of a struggle; after all, that's why most people visit me and my website. I know only too well how easy it is to stumble on life's highways and byways, to feel a bit lost and unsure of which road to take. Or perhaps I wrote them in order to let others know that I was still alive and working. Now that I come to think of it, it was probably a bit of both.

Here they are, presented in a form that will allow you to read a different column every week of the year. You might like to dip into them, beginning with the month and week you are in as you read this, or perhaps you'd like to read them through from start to finish, but I think you'll need to pause quite often if you do it this way. You might like to take them out occasionally, when the going gets tough and reflect for a few moments to consider just where you are in your life's journey. Whichever way you choose to read is exactly the right way for you.

Those who come to see me in my role as a psychotherapist have no doubt that I am still living, and there are enough of them to fill my appointment book for weeks in advance and to keep me very busy indeed. And this is just the way I like it. There are few greater joys in this life than seeing someone change before your own eyes and to know that you have played some small part in their transformation.

But there must be others, judging by the emails I get and the number of hits my website receives, who will never come to see me, and so we will never meet, either because they live in some other part of the world, or for reasons that I will never know; people who seem to enjoy my writings — the musings of a therapist and above all, of a person, a human being, just like them.

For all of these people, and for you, dear reader, I offer this little book. I hope that somewhere inside you will find what you need, a gentle reminder of all that you are and of all that you can be.

**Peter Field**

# Standing on the Edge

❦

Here we are. The earth has taken one more full circle around the sun and the days of the seasons have come and gone.

The old year is behind us now, but its memories and its teachings remain.

They are a part of us, just as the coming days and the coming seasons will so very soon become part of who we are, pages and chapters in the story that is our life.

And at this time, it's good to reflect. It's good to stop and to become aware of how very fortunate we really are to be here, paused for the briefest of moments on the edge of a whole new year: A year packed with fresh days and fresh seasons yet to be lived.

In this we are all equal. Each of us is here, standing before this gift that is a new year. In it there will be just 365 days and not a single moment more.

We do not have forever. Even our longings have limits.

One year from now how will you remember this New Year? What decisions will you have made and remained loyal to? How will you have moved forward and grown?

What will you have become that you are not today?

**Make up your mind now that this year will be different from all the others.** Let this be the year that you find some grass on which to go barefoot — and what the heck if people are watching; learn something new, something that is not connected with your work or with making money; do something nice, something kind for another person without letting on that it was you who did it.

Decide that this will be the year when you reach out beyond your imaginary limits and fears; the year you learn to grow and to be more fully and spontaneously you.

If there is something inside that has been holding you back, take this opportunity to do something about it.

Why not let this New Year be lived in the awareness that **you are so much more than the experiences through which you have passed?** This could be the year when you finally allow yourself to see that you are *not* your past.

You really do have choices, yet those choices only become available when you realise that they are there — and then decide to do something about it.

Why not begin right now? There really is no better time.

Look ahead to the coming year and see yourself becoming the person you want to become. Then make up your mind to be that person, the person you were really born to be, the person that you really are deep inside.

There is no hidden treasure of greater value than the year that is now here with you. It truly is priceless and it will not come again.

It's up to you now to take this gift, this New Year, and to make it great.

Go on, take courage — you know you can do it!

*'The object of a New Year is not that we should have a new year.
It is that we should have a new soul'*
**G. K. Chesterton**

# Dust Off Your Dreams

❦

Already a week has passed as we move forward into this brand new year. This is a time of new beginnings; the time when you really can begin to live the life that you truly do deserve.

Do you have your goals fixed, your dreams set firmly in your mind's eye?

You know that we human beings need goals to motivate and dreams to inspire us. Don't be afraid to dream big. That old saying is as meaningful today as when it was first spoken: *Dreams really do come true.*

If your dreams have been dashed to pieces in the past, say goodbye to them now and be grateful for them. They were not wasted. Didn't they spur you on and motivate you as you dreamt them? So what if morning came too soon? That's the job of mornings, to tell us to pick ourselves up and get on with our day.

Your dreams are still there, somewhere inside you. They may well have changed, because you're wiser and more experienced now, and because that's the nature of dreams, but they're still there, waiting. Get them out and dust them off.

Let this be the year when you put your dreams into action.

What needs to be changed in your life in order for your dreams to come true? What needs to be done in order for you to move forward and grow? What limiting beliefs are stopping you from shining? **Whatever it is it's within your power to change and there's no better time to begin than right now.**

Anything is within your reach if you're prepared to put forth the effort, to pay the price — and for your dreams to become reality it *will* take work.

Don't hold back. Give the best of yourself in everything you touch, everything you do. Be the very best you that you can possibly be, and don't allow yourself to settle for anything less. Give more than is expected but don't forget to keep enough for yourself. Do it with a willing heart and you will be amazed at the rewards that will come your way.

Accept this feast now laid before you, this brand new year, add a pinch of courage and take a great big bite. Make that big leap. Start working today on those changes that need to be made and you'll see — your dreams really can come true.

> *'The best way to make your dreams come true*
> *is to wake up...'*
> **Paul Valéry**

# Renewal

∾

Another brand new week has arrived; another brand new day has dawned. Reach out and grab it while it's here. Choose to live it now.

All your yesterdays are behind you and now you can use them to propel yourself forward. You are wiser now, more experienced, and now you have this great opportunity to begin afresh.

Let this be the Day of New Beginnings, the day when you really do start to make your dreams come true. Don't let it slip through your fingers.

What better time is there to let go of the past and move forward? Whatever your personal history has been, if you choose to you can leave it behind now. And if you're wise that's just what you'll do.

Have you succeeded at something? If so, then well done! But the race is not over and now's not the time to rest on your laurels.

Have your efforts met with failure? Then you've learned what works and what doesn't. It's time to pick yourself up now and get back in the saddle.

You made mistakes in the past? Yes, perhaps you did. But have you ever met anyone who did not make mistakes, both big and small?

I never have.

The important thing to remember is that **you are not your mistakes**, they were things you did or that you failed to do, but they are not who you are and they never were.

You are you — even if you do not yet fully understand just who this you is.

The wise person understands that their mistakes, like their past, are there for a reason. They are there to instruct and to teach, but they were never meant to be lived in, to be rehashed endlessly, over and over again.

No matter what your past has held it does not need to dictate your future. You have the power to begin afresh, to change. You can write a brand new chapter in the book of your life and if you have not already begun then there is no better time to begin than right now.

So many people had to live, to pass before, in order for you to be here today. Just like you and me, they were gifted with new years, with new days, with hopes and with dreams.

Do not squander and waste this gift. Grasp this new and fresh chance you have been given. Is there any better time to live?

You are here now for a reason; even if that reason is not clear to you. You are at the start of something big. It's called the rest of your life.

Go ahead: **Move forward with confidence now.** After all, no one can do it for you.

This is your life and only you can live it.

> *'We must be willing to let go of the life we have planned,*
> *so as to accept the life that is waiting for us…'*
> **Joseph Campbell**

# The Real News

~

The crisp mornings and frosty nights of this last week in January remind us that we are again in the middle of winter. And this particular winter sees our world once more passing through unsettling times.

In so many regions, and in so many hearts, peace has given way to war and love has been usurped by hatred.

The newscasts and the newspapers inform and remind us of the economic uncertainty in which we find ourselves and the uneasiness that this creates is so often reflected in the faces of the people who come to see me.

Of course, no one I meet expects me to have any kind of solution to wars or to be able to solve the economic quagmire that illusion and greed has brought us to.

I am, after all, a therapist, and not a political advisor or military strategist.

People do not visit me in order to directly secure their job or to bank their money.

No, people come to the therapist because they have had enough of feeling stuck or powerless and because they feel the need to *do* something about it. They come because they want to move on with their lives and they are ready for change.

And only then can I help them.

We know that the news media will never tire of reminding us that there is reason to fear. It will never be short of stories that describe and graphically delineate the rise of hatred and uncertainty in the world.

But sometimes what is overlooked is the incontrovertible fact that despite all the reasons to fear, there are even more reasons for courage. Despite all the hatred in the world, there is more to be loved than hated — and there always will be.

Yes, we need to be aware of what is happening around and about us, what is happening in the world. But that does not mean that we are powerless puppets and that we can do nothing.

There is not a single one of us that was born to be a marionette, or a victim.

Even in the midst of uncertainty and change, we have a say in our own destiny. Once we feel the need to do something all that remains is to know that we can.

**See yourself as moving forward** and that will automatically become the direction in which you move.

You have it within you to cope. **You have the ability to steer your own course and weather any storm.**

Today your life begins all over again. The things you choose to do now and the actions that you take have the power to transform your life, your work, your relationships, your business and your world.

Even in the winter and in the most unsettling of times, you have it within yourself to move forward into stability and growth. You have even the ability to help not only yourself, but also others whom you meet on your journey.

The real news is that you have it within you to fully live the wonderful gift that is your life.

*'What lies behind us and what lies before us are small matters compared to what lies within us'*
**Ralph Waldo Emerson**

# Take this Jewel

❧

February is here! Just twenty eight brief days — with an extra one thrown in for good luck if it's a leap year — and then it will be gone, never to return…

With each day there will be challenges to be faced, just as there will be joy to be experienced.

Along with the discoveries there may well be disappointments. Mixed right in with the light there may well be dark. But whatever comes your way brings with it an opportunity to learn and to grow.

In each experience there is a lesson and there is little doubt that some lessons will be easier to learn than others. But we cannot choose to learn only from the easy experiences: In fact, it's often the more difficult and uncomfortable experiences that have more to teach us.

If we are to really learn life's lessons we need to open our minds to *all* experience, because in each experience there is something to be learned, something to be gained.

The truth is that each single day brings with it its own special opportunity, its own special message. And all we need to do is listen; because when we allow ourselves to listen we become open to new learning.

If things are going well for you right now, then keep right on doing what you're doing because you're doing something right. Life will tell you when you need to change course.

If things are difficult then **take a step back** instead of becoming totally overwhelmed by what is happening. Step outside the worry, the anxiety or the boredom, the chaos or the cacophony. Pause for a moment and pretend that those things belong to someone else, someone who has come to you for advice.

How can you best help that person?

Is it helpful if you too begin to worry, become really anxious or bored? How can you really listen when you are adding to the clamour, the commotion?

Take that step back and choose to look at the whole, not just at a part. Ask yourself if you truly do need to jump to that conclusion, see things in that particular way. Is it really as bad as it seems? You've been in rough waters before and you made it through the storm.

Isn't there a bigger picture, a larger reason behind it all? It doesn't need to be clear or apparent at this moment in time. Just step outside of that judgmental self, look with your heart and you will begin to see and to understand.

Then go one step further and consider how you can make use of this understanding.

Listen carefully now and you will hear the clock that is ticking. All too soon February will be gone. Why not **take each and every minute of these days and really live it?** Treat it like the precious jewel that it really is; polish it, and let it sparkle and shine.

Do this and your joy will come.

*'Your time is limited,*
*don't waste it living someone else's life'*
**Steve Jobs, Apple Inc.**

# Beating the Valentine's Day Blues

 ～

Wasn't it only yesterday we were buying those Christmas and New Year's cards? And now it's February and along comes Valentine's Day, with its romantic hopes and expectations. Love it or loath it, Valentine's Day is here to stay.

Not everyone loves it, of course. Many people have fallen for the ads and the commercial interests that imply they're out of sync, that something might be wrong with them if they're not in a romantic relationship, giving or receiving those cards, chocolates and flowers.

Single people can find themselves having to deal with really uncomfortable feelings for not having their own special Valentine at this time of year.

If you've received a Valentine then enjoy it. Appreciate it for what it is — an expression of someone's affection, but don't go overboard on those chocolates!

If you're feeling left out, with no Valentine in your life, then don't let the Valentine's Day Blues get to you.

The key to beating it lies in the realisation that not being in a romantic relationship at the moment is not the end of the world. In fact, it might be a beginning — provided you use your feelings in a positive way.

Dwelling on the negative is, after all, a self-defeating exercise. The truth is that we tend to get what we focus on. This is known as the 'Law of Focus'. Every time we focus on the negative, we are giving the subconscious mind instructions to create those things.

The solution really isn't that difficult to come by. Instead of beating yourself up, give yourself a pat on the back for meeting the many challenges single life can deliver.

Here are three tips for beating the Valentine's Day Blues:

1) *Count what you have, not what you don't have.* Acknowledge that you are a person who is growing, learning and becoming more self-sufficient all the time. You've already accomplished a lot — and you're capable of achieving even more.

2) *Focus on where you're going.* If it's a romantic relationship you're after, use Valentine's Day to motivate you to do something about it. Reach out. Join a club, an association of like-minded people, exercise. If you're waiting for something to happen, don't put your life on the back burner until it does. Prince Charming and Fairy Godmothers belong in children's stories, not in the real world. So…

3) *Get real.* Don't get sucked in by those idealised advertising images. The best way to do this is by developing a strong, positive self-image. The better you feel about yourself, the less you'll be bothered by artificial pressures. And few things are more attractive than confidence!

When you **focus on what's there more than on what's not** there, on where you're going rather than on where you've been, then you'll seize this day and move forward.

Just remember, you don't need those commercial pressures and clever advertising campaigns to tell you you're worth it. The truth is that you really are.

Get out there now and let your light shine!

*'Love yourself first and everything else falls into line. You really have to love yourself to get anything done in this world'*
**Lucille Ball**

# The Path of Change

〜

E ach day I welcome clients into my office who come to see me for a host of different reasons. Some want to lose weight, kick a habit, or end an addiction. Others want to rid themselves of fears and negative feelings that have plagued them for years. Still others are depressed or stuck and feeling really unhappy about the direction their lives have taken.

But no matter what reason they come to see me, all of my clients have one thing in common — they have come to the point in their lives where they really want to change. And they have decided to do something about it.

Writing in his book *Man's Search for Meaning*, Auschwitz survivor and psychiatrist Victor Frankl observed: **'When we are no longer able to change a situation, we are challenged to change ourselves'**.

And so the work begins, and as long as there is genuine commitment, then before too long, change takes place. Yet so often it happens in ways that we may not have anticipated.

You see, it can sometimes take a little while to notice the really positive changes that are taking place within us. This is because real change happens on such a profound level, becoming an integral part of who we are and how we respond. It just feels so natural.

Many times we notice change only after the event — when we've put the phone down and realised that we reacted in an entirely different way, for example, or when we sail smoothly through a situation that would previously have upset, angered or frustrated us. Or maybe it's only when we're about to sleep and we realise that we just haven't felt like compulsively snacking or emotionally eating all day.

The simple fact is that true change doesn't happen simply on an abstract, intellectual level. It happens on an emotional, feeling one. After all, it's the way we *feel* that tells us what's really happening inside us. It's the way we feel that tells us how we're really doing.

The changes you make need to be authentic changes, not facades, or a ruse designed to fool someone. Though real change certainly does influence external things, it is not on the outside that the change takes place.

Real change is something that is made deep down… within yourself.

Perhaps the American philosopher Henry David Thoreau best summed it up when he said: 'Things do not change — we change'.

A good therapist can certainly facilitate and be a catalyst for change, but the real therapist is Life. If you have lived then you've already been in therapy and so you can use what you've learned. Ultimately, it is you who make the changes in your life and you who deserve the credit.

Take a look in your internal mirror and ask yourself if you have changed and if that change is really for the better. If the answer is 'Yes', then well done! You're moving forward and you're heading in exactly the right direction for you.

If the answer is 'No', then decide now to do something about it. You owe it to yourself to live *your* life. **Put your foot firmly on the path of change and start walking,** then pull up that anchor and set sail.

You just might be surprised at how far you can travel, how much you can change.

> 'We cannot discover new oceans unless we have the courage
> to lose sight of the shore'
> **André Gide**

# Put on Your Dancing Shoes

~

Have you noticed that life seems to have become even more hurried lately?

If not, then maybe it means you're in step with your reality, dancing in time with the rhythm of your life. Make sure you dance with your heart as well as your feet and you'll have a ball.

Sometimes, though, it seems to take more and more energy simply to stay in the same place. All that rushing around may even have had you dragging your feet.

If you've been feeling somehow stuck and faded, then now's your chance to get out of that rut and do something about it.

When we feel flat it means we need to consider what we're doing and where we're really going. Has life become mere routine, an endless march with each day a simple repetition of the previous one?

It doesn't have to be that way. It's within your power to change things.

If you're feeling a bit down and depleted, as if you're running on empty, then maybe that's just the push you need. You know that if you keep right on doing what you've always done, then you'll get what you've always got, so maybe that feeling is trying to tell you something important.

Perhaps it's there to tell you how to move forward and grow. Maybe you need to take off your heavy work boots and put on those dancing shoes.

Maybe it's time to dance to a different tune.

If you're just not happy with where you are right now, then take a quick step back and look at where you really want to be. **See the life you really want to live and have the courage to go after it.** Let go of those limits you've placed on yourself. The courage you need is already there, inside you, just waiting for you to use.

Isn't now the time to reach down and bring it out? After all, if appetite grows with the eating, then courage grows with the doing. It might mean breaking with the past, and even with some of the people who have been holding you back. You might have to make a fresh, new start, but it will be worth it.

Find something to be passionate about, something that makes your heart sing, your spirit dance. You'll know what this is because it will not drag you down — it will energise you. Then reach into that passion; let it guide you and give you purpose.

It might mean taking a bit of a risk; it will mean finding that bit of courage, but those things are far less costly than regret. This is your life. Treat it as if it's the only one you have and you won't go far wrong.

Inside you is your passion, mix it with a little courage, give it rein and it will dance you to where the music is. It will take you to where you need to be.

*'Those who danced were thought to be quite insane*
*by those who could not hear the music…'*
**Friedrich Nietzsche (attrib.)**

# The Train We Ride

~

J ust last week I was travelling by train from London to Birmingham and found myself in a seat that faced backwards.

Gazing out of the window, I enjoyed seeing the world through which I had passed simply speeding by.

Not a very new experience, of course. At one time or another most of us have travelled with our backs to the direction in which we were going.

But this time a novel thought occurred to me...

What if we could live our lives backwards? Wouldn't it be simple to avoid mistakes? We might easily look back on our mistakes, see them coming and then avoid them.

We might even be able to move in another direction.

But in the real world — the world in which we live — time moves forward, not backward and avoiding mistakes isn't nearly as easy as gazing retrospectively from a train window.

And because of this, the only possible way to avoid making mistakes is to avoid making anything, to avoid taking any kind of action whatsoever.

Yet this, of course, besides being an impossibility, would be one of the greatest mistakes we could make.

Because without our mistakes, we would remain as we were. We would not grow. We would not learn. We would not move forward.

In the vocabulary of psychology, mistakes are called 'successive approximations'. Whether we are learning to ride a bicycle, read, or navigate life's course, through successively approximating the correct result, we can eventually learn to get it right.

The fact is that in order to grow, to learn and to move forward, we need to make mistakes, we need to 'successively approximate'. This doesn't mean that we should seek out mistakes, of course: They will come anyway.

After all, even the wisest person amongst us will make mistakes.

The real wisdom comes in learning from our mistakes — and then forgiving ourselves for those mistakes.

When we do that we become free to move forward with our lives.

If you find yourself clinging to past mistakes; if you feel lost, anxious and fed up; if you are confused and unhappy, then there really is something you can do about it.

The train you are riding will take you even deeper into the darkest of tunnels, if you allow it to. In fact, if you wait long enough, it will take you all the way to the cemetery. But you can choose to get off that train at any time you like. You can take another train, one that will take you to the mountaintop.

You are not powerless.

**It is within your power to choose the train you are riding on.** It is within your power to live your life in a positive, forward moving direction.

Why not get up and change trains now?

There really is no better time to get your life back on the right track!

> *'Life can only be understood backwards,*
> *but it must be lived forwards'*
> **Søren Kierkegaard**

# The Stillness Within

With today's uncertain climate and with change happening so rapidly all around us, it can easily feel as if we're running simply to stay in the same place.

When everything about us is in flux and turmoil it's easy to lose our own balance, letting our world and some of the people we share it with take us away from ourselves and from who we really are.

It's easy to feel lost.

Sometimes it can feel as if we're spending all our time and energy just shoring things up, mending fences, securing those boundaries that keep us safe and that hold our world together.

But sometimes, too, it can be those very boundaries that are holding us back and stopping us from being who we can be, who we were really born to be. Sometimes it is our own boundaries, the ones that we have placed on ourselves that limit our growth and our progress.

One thing I know is that no one *is* his or her boundaries. No one is the limit that they themselves have placed on their reality.

**Within you is the power to change your life.** You *can* let go of those feelings that separate you from you. No matter how lost you feel you are, no matter how lost you may have been, you can come back home to yourself. You can allow yourself to be you — even if you've lost sight of who you truly are.

If you have strayed away from yourself then maybe it's time to come back home.

Perhaps it's time to let go of all those out-dated, learned beliefs that stop you from shining. Time to let go of the pretence that is preventing you from moving on with your life. You may have fooled others, but isn't it hard having to keep it up?

If all that running is simply taking you farther and farther away from yourself then maybe it's time to slow down, stop running and be still for a while.

After all, just as there is a time to do, so there is a time to be.

Take the time to be.

There is a still and peaceful place within you that exists beyond anxiety and fear, beyond anger, guilt or need. In this place there is no need to do. It is a place where peace awaits you.

If that which once made you stand out is now separating you from you and from your own inner peace, then take the time to be. Separate yourself from all that is without and spend some time within.

The world and all the people in it will still be here, but you will see it with different eyes. After all, those things are not you and they never were you.

The stillness and peace you seek is there within, awaiting you.

And all you need do is to stop doing and begin to simply be.

*'There is more to life than increasing its speed...'*
**Mahatma Gandhi**

# Transforming the Impossible

$\sim$

A couple of weeks ago I was again invited to talk on BBC Radio. This time the subject was phobias. With the warm and spontaneous Mollie Green guest hosting the morning show, I was introduced to a lovely young news reporter called Louisa.

With hundreds of thousands of people listening, Louisa bravely told us of her terrible fear, one that she had experienced for as long as she could remember.

Eyes welling up, and visibly upset, she spoke courageously of her awful, incapacitating phobia. It was one she had experienced for as long as she could remember. Louisa was terrified of *stickers*.

Before you smile, consider this — who has not in some way or another been afraid of something? Fear is fear. It does not need to be rational in order for us to feel it.

For Louisa, buying fruit, for example, was an absolute nightmare because so much produce came with a sticker on it. Going to a concert was a major ordeal since staff so often tried to place a sticker on her as she entered. Stickers appeared to be everywhere from shops and concerts to the walls of the BBC where she worked!

Valiantly, Louisa told us how, whenever she encountered a sticker, her heart would pound, nausea rising within, as an almost overwhelming fear and panic gripped her, telling her to flee just as fast as her legs could carry her.

She could not even eat apple pie in a restaurant for fear that the apples used might once have touched stickers or had stickers on them!

You see, though she was not yet consciously aware of it, since Louisa was three years old, her mind had accepted the belief that she could not handle stickers of any kind, and from that moment on this belief had become part and parcel of the life she was forced to live.

She told herself that she could not, her subconscious mind had accepted this belief, and so this belief automatically became her reality.

Happily, Louisa accompanied me back to my office following the show, and with advanced hypnotherapy we completely removed her terrible, incapacitating fear. She returned to the BBC absolutely beaming, an apple sticker stuck proudly and mischievously to her forehead. She is free to live her life without that fear now. She is free now to be her wonderful self.

Though Louisa's fear of stickers was somewhat rare, her case is far from unique.

So many of us have told ourselves that there are things we simply cannot do. So many of us settle for and live lives full of upset, anxiety or fear, lives in which the possible feels impossible.

Pause for just a moment and ask yourself a simple question: What have you told yourself that you cannot do?

Whatever it is, it is not true: **If it is humanly possible, then you can do it. You can change your life!**

Just what is necessary in order to transform the impossible into the possible? Well, all it takes is a change in your thinking. Every single doubt you have is kept alive by your own thoughts. And you were not born to be the victim of your own — or of anyone else's — thoughts or beliefs.

Yes, setting yourself free takes effort. If Louisa had not made the effort to enter into hypnotherapy, then she would not have changed and her awful fear would have remained her reality.

Achievement takes effort, making that first step isn't always easy, yet neither is poverty, or fear, or misery, or feeling terrible about yourself.

The truth is that you already have all that you need to change. It's right there inside you. And it's there in abundance. Those positive opportunities really are there, they are already in your life, and they can overpower any limitations.

This is your life and there truly is no need to waste it. It's up to you now to take that first step.

*'Impossible is not fact, it's opinion'*
**Muhammad Ali**

# Time for Fun

~

The man about to recline in my therapy chair had a dejected look about him. 'I never have any fun!' he sighed.

'What do you think might be stopping you from having more fun?' I asked.

'I know it's me', he said. 'I have everything I need — a good home, nice wife, a good job, so I'm the one who's stopping me, but I just don't know how to put it right.'

'Perhaps all that's needed is for you to give yourself permission', I said. 'Let's see how you can do that.' And our work began.

What was really needed was for this man to *allow* himself to be what he really wanted to be.

If we really want to be comfortable in our own skin, then above all we need to give ourselves permission to be happy and to have fun. We need to let go of the idea that fun is wrong. It really is OK to be happy.

Life really doesn't need to be all seriousness and industry. Taking the time to enjoy ourselves is crucial if we are to live a life of balance and inner joy.

After all, there is a time to do and a time to be.

What kind of thing can you do in order to be more fully you and have fun?

How about discovering or rediscovering your passion for life itself? Why not become like a child, full of curiosity, looking at the world with fresh eyes that see and feel its wonder?

Take the advice you might give to another: Splash through puddles and turn your face up to the rain — after all, it's only water you've been hiding from all these years; watch a dog wag his tail or marvel at the purring of a cat; travel to where you can see the sun set over water or sink behind the hilltops. Go somewhere you have never been before and do something you've never done. Spend some time with the very old and with the very young. Smile at someone you've never met and notice how you feel. If it feels strange, then don't worry, just keep on smiling and you'll get used to it.

Give of yourself, but don't forget to keep something back for yourself. Do whatever it takes to be happy without impressing others — recognise that your joy is already there, inside you. Enjoy the privilege of being alive. **Live the miracle.** In life we really do have choices, and realising this simple truth is key to the art of living.

Though you may not always be able to control what happens to you, **you can learn to control the way in which you respond to the things that happen to you.**

We can abnegate responsibility for ourselves, play the victim, choose to be marionettes, our strings pulled by the past, by external events or by other people, or we can choose to take back control, acting and not reacting, becoming responsible for our own role in our own life.

Yes, perhaps there are changes to be made, but only we can make them.

We can choose to view the changes that we need to make as a troublesome burden, something we would do only grudgingly, or we can choose to see them as a kind of fresh adventure, an exciting revolution in the way we live and feel. The choice really is ours.

**The choice really is yours.**

*'I never lose sight of the fact that just being is fun...'*
**Katharine Hepburn**

# Just Begin

~

S pring is almost upon us and those of us living in the UK have already set our clocks forward by an hour in line with daylight saving time.

This doesn't mean that we have any less or any more time to spend, of course.

A second is still a second and a breath is still a breath in each of our lives.

Even with that adjustment to the clocks, there is not one moment more or one moment less available to any of us.

Yet it is the way we use those moments that determines the course of our lives.

Indeed, the way we spend our moments is the way we spend our lives, just as the way that we do anything tends to be the way we do everything.

Even as you read this, the clock is ticking. None of us, after all, have forever.

**What you do now has the power to completely change your life.** But the simple truth is that it isn't enough to think about it. You need to *do* it.

The smallest action has the power to change your world because the smallest action has much more power than even the best thought out intention.

If we are perceptive, we will see that sometimes life invites us to take a little leap of faith; it asks us to trust it enough to take a chance and jump into the unknown.

Yes, the unknown can be scary. We can allow fear to freeze and block us, to bring us to a grinding halt, or we can use that fear as a springboard to take action and to move us forward.

Action, after all, has the power to conquer fear. And courage comes with the doing.

Start from where you are, not from where you'd like to be — though **keep where you want to be firmly in mind.**

Be ruthlessly honest with yourself. Acknowledge where you are at the present time and then begin to head in the direction of the place where you need to go.

All it takes is to get up and begin — and then keep on with that beginning. Venture out of your zone of comfort. Make that telephone call. Send that email. Knock on that door. Shake that hand. Smile that smile. Keep right on and your courage and confidence will grow with each step you take.

It really doesn't matter how far behind you feel yourself to be, what matters is that you begin to move forward.

**Real success, after all, depends not on your position, but on your disposition. It depends on your direction and your attitude.**

The really important thing is to begin.

> *'What saves a person is to take a step —*
> *then another step'*
> **Antoine De Saint-Exupery**

# The Colour of Spring

C olour is returning to our world. All around us the greys, blacks and whites are giving way to the vibrant greens and yellows of daffodils and primroses. Blossoms and buds are busy singing out, as winter once more fades into a memory.

Indeed, there is a sense that the whole world of nature is being renewed, ending its hibernation, becoming reborn.

Almost paradoxically, though, April is also the month that finds many people feeling blue and struggling with difficult feelings — feelings of melancholy and downheartedness. For some, as the poet said, April truly is the cruellest month.

But what is it about April and spring that can leave so many feeling down and depressed?

Well, when the external world lacks colour and the sky is grey, as it so often is in winter, then it's as if we have a justification, a rationalization for feeling down. We have an almost tangible explanation for feeling 'under the weather'. Yet when these depressed feelings persist inside us, and all around us we see that the whole world is being renewed and starting afresh, then we can all too easily fall even deeper into the dumps and the gloom of melancholy.

It's almost as though spring is a stark measure, a yardstick that plainly points to the distance between how we think we *should* feel and how we really *do* feel.

And this, of course, is why we have rituals such as spring-cleaning.

Something inside us knows that as we clean away the dust and the cobwebs from our personal space, we are symbolically dusting within, sweeping out some of our internal cobwebs, too. Indeed, giving our personal environment a thorough cleansing provides us with a sense of control and empowerment that can cheer and brighten things, inside and out.

If you're feeling blue or melancholy because spring is here, then there really is no need to sit back and play victim to the seasons. Here are just a couple of things that you can begin to do right away in order to empower yourself and put your house back in order:

- *Focus on positive self-talk.* What begins in your mind ends up in your life. Everything you say to yourself about yourself is a message to your subconscious mind to make whatever you tell yourself come true. Put things into the positive. By monitoring self-talk and thinking continually of the way you would most like to be, your reality will reliably fall in line.

- *Listen to your feelings.* When you experience doubt, feel fear, or anger, or frustration, or sadness, listen to what the feeling is trying to tell you. Once you've identified the cause of the feeling, do something about it. Denying it or attempting to distract yourself from it by overeating, drinking, popping pills or any number of other self-defeating strategies simply won't help for long because sooner or later the feeling will return with a vengeance, leaving you as uncomfortable as ever.

- *Learn a new skill or develop a fresh interest.* Learn self-hypnosis or meditation; begin a regular exercise regime — walking, or taking up a sport, or perhaps joining a gym and making sure you stick with it. Challenge yourself to learn something new, whether by attending a course at your local college or perhaps joining an Internet group of others whose interests you share. You could even teach something that you already know something about to others.

But the very best way to feel better is to reach out and help someone else, someone less fortunate than you. Do this and you'll put spring where it really belongs — in your step.

No one was born to feel bad about themselves or about their life. Each and every one of us has the power to become what we were meant to be — a whole person, a life-affirming person, a person who feels good about him or herself, a human being who appreciates the gift of life and isn't afraid to be its vehicle, to express and enjoy it.

I hope you will **keep your life focused on your most treasured dreams,** tuned to your brilliant possibilities. And who knows, maybe we'll meet — in my office or out somewhere looking at those wonderful spring blossoms.

*'Spring is sooner recognised by plants than by men'*
**Chinese Proverb**

# Responsibility

~

Is there something in your life that is still holding you back, something that you still need to change?

If there is then you are certainly not alone.

Very few people are completely satisfied with every aspect of their lives. Most of us would like to change something or other — if only we could.

Some of us buy flashy cars or a new wardrobe of clothes in the hope that we can change our life. Others change jobs, separate from family, move house, get divorced or even emigrate in an attempt to bring about the change that they believe they need in order to feel better.

Practically everyone who comes to see me in my work as a therapist is there because they want to change.

Some hope that I can change *for* them, that change is something that can be done *to* them, but I quickly explain that this, sadly, is not possible.

Though I am a therapist who specialises in helping people to change, the only person I can really change is myself.

Only when a person is willing to accept responsibility for his or her own change can I truly help them to change. Only then can real and affirmative change truly be brought about.

With responsibility comes a greater degree of control, and with this control comes the freedom to fulfil our own potential and to move forward into the better life that we are capable of living.

Regardless of the past and what may or may not have happened in that past, no matter who was to blame or who was innocent, we own it now.

It is ours now and because it is ours then we can do whatever we wish with it.

**We can even let it go.**

Yes, you can choose to hold onto it, continue to nurse the grudges and luxuriate in the resentments; you can point your finger and righteously feel sorry for yourself; you can stew in feelings of anger or guilt, but what will this bring you? It will bring you more of the same, but it will not bring you the change that you need and deserve.

There is another way, a better way.

When we take responsibility for our life then we take back control over it. **With responsibility we automatically become director of our own life, and so master of our own future.**

Isn't responsibility a small price to pay for something as important and as valuable as that?

*'Responsibility is the price of freedom'*
**Elbert Hubbard**

# The Lottery

~

J ust last week the ever-bubbly receptionist at my practice mislaid the lottery ticket she had bought and was turning everything upside down and inside out looking for it when I arrived.

She seemed convinced that she'd lost the winning ticket.

Already she'd retraced her steps back to the newsagent where she'd bought it, but to no avail.

It turned up later, of course, but only after she'd re-checked the results and found that it wasn't the winning ticket after all. Something in me couldn't resist a wry little smile.

What would have happened if she had really won? Would it have been like every wonderful birthday she ever had all rolled into one — only to be snatched away from her?

So many of the people I meet are like that lovely receptionist, waiting for the right ticket, the big win, something external that will come along and change their life forever.

But few realise that in life's lottery they have already won, and they've won simply because they're alive. Perhaps now is a good time to take a step back and realise this.

There really is no better time than right now to appreciate life for what it is, what it always was and always will be — a wonderful unfolding mystery to be lived and not a problem or a puzzle to be solved.

Filled with darkness and light, joy and sorrow; miraculous at times, disappointing at others; life brings with it the most beautiful of rewards and sometimes, too, the deepest, most impenetrable of losses.

As long as we draw breath, these things will be somewhere there, more constant than any companion, more plentiful than winning lottery tickets.

Too often we want life to change, to be something other than it is. We want it to be the way we want it to be, even though we know deep down inside that it can only ever be the way that it is.

It is we who must change, we who *will* change, and whether we change for the better or for the worse is really down to us and to the choices we ourselves make.

We may at times feel impelled, but we are never truly compelled. We are given choices, we are free to select the winning combination, but we become the choices that we make and we alone are the authors of our own story.

Stipulate your terms, write out your contract if you like, but don't expect life to sign it. Its simple and honest offer is always there, on the table, and you can take it up any time you like: **Live while you have life**.

Good therapy really can greatly help you on your journey, clearing the debris of the past, making way for the now. It can improve your vision for the future, and give you compass and rudder to use as you journey on. But you can also be your own physician as you work with the greatest therapist of all — Life.

Never forget that this is your life, and when all is said and done **only you can make it work.**

Now, about that winning lottery ticket…

*'I've learned that you don't have to win first place to win…'*
**Kim Zmeska**

# Your Ship Awaits You

~

So many people seek therapeutic help because they feel that they have come to the end of their tether and they're all at sea.

For them, life's sparkle seems to have faded, and they are left — at whatever age — feeling old and tired.

Often clients report having tried a whole range of strategies in order to feel better. Sometimes they reel off a list of self-help books, of therapies and therapists they have consulted before arriving at my office.

Yet still they feel stuck. Still they are hurting.

They have simply had enough of feeling bad about themselves and their lives and they recognise that they cannot continue as they are; that they really must do something about it.

Problems must be worked through. They just don't evaporate with wishful thinking.

Only when this understanding is in place can things really begin to change.

Perhaps now is the time to look clearly at your life. Do you think you're too old or too late or too stuck in the past? Are you tired of feeling like you've missed the boat or of simply hanging around hoping that your ship will one day come in?

If so, you are wrong.

The truth is that your ship already awaits you. **You are in exactly the right time and place to make real and positive changes in your life**

**and in your world.** You are in exactly the right position to become the 'you' that your life wants you to be.

Yes, you may well have made mistakes; you may know all about regret; you may have been hurt and become weary, but still life holds an abundance of possibilities for you.

If you feel that you have lost your direction, do not despair. Experience teaches that so many of those who truly found their way did so only after they had first admitted that they had lost it. I know this because it was true for me, too.

At the end of our tether and in the despair of defeat we were gifted with the humility necessary to understand what had been hidden, and with this understanding we were able to move forward.

From the ashes of defeat came rebirth and true renewal.

Your life's journey is not yet over — not by a long shot. If you have had a wonderful past then it is time to build on this and move on now. If you have had a terrible, painful past then it is time for you to move on now.

The reality is that you were born to live your life with enthusiasm and with joy — you really can be the captain of your ship.

The only thing that can stop you from being you is you.

*'You may have a fresh start any moment you choose.*
*This thing that we call 'failure' is not the falling down,*
*but the staying down'*
**Mary Pickford**

# The Certain Uncertainty
# of Change

⌒

As you read this you are already changing. Though you may not notice that change, it is already taking place.

Change is the one certain, cardinal law of life, something that happens without our permission and often without our conscious awareness.

As a therapist, the work that I do has everything to do with change. People come to see me because they know they need to change, but they do not know how.

Some have become fearful of change because their past has brought them the kind of change that they really did not expect or want, and this fear has fed into feelings of insecurity.

We all know that **change must come**, but we also know that the nature of that change is uncertain. It is this sense of uncertainty that fuels so much unnecessary anxiety.

Resisting change, or demanding change on our terms, we become more anxious and fearful, turning life's uncertainty into our insecurity.

Yet uncertainty does not have to mean insecurity.

When we allow ourselves to accept change and take that step further, learning to *embrace* it, placing our faith in life itself, then we ourselves change in a positive way; our very nature is somehow altered.

We have become flexible and adaptable enough to handle whatever life brings our way, to roll with the punches and to ride life's wonderful wave to wherever it takes us.

We become more secure in ourselves and so life becomes easier and richer.

Something unexpected may very well happen today, or if not today then tomorrow. Change will come and you can choose to worry about it or you can choose to look forward to it as part of the disclosing miracle of existence.

When we can see life's uncertainty as part of life's wonderful adventure, then our insecurity vanishes and we are freed to live as we were meant to live, secure in the change that life will surely bring.

*'To be uncertain is to be uncomfortable,*
*but to be certain is to be ridiculous…'*
**Chinese Proverb**

# Lighting a Candle

~

May is finally here and summer — well, it's just a skip away. And there's no doubt that these longer, light-filled days can have a wonderful, uplifting effect on the spirit.

Though night-time certainly has its place, given the chance, most of us would prefer to live in the light, rather than stumble in the darkness.

Light and darkness, of course, are not simple, external qualities. They're also metaphors for what's happening inside us, on an emotional level. Indeed, people so often come to the therapist because they've simply had enough of cursing the darkness. And they've decided to do something about it.

So many of us have grown up learning how to be self-critical. After all, it's easy to beat yourself up about real or imagined mistakes you make or have made.

Having learned to feel bad about things we believe — or have been taught to believe — are bad, we learn to internalise these negative feelings, replaying them over and over again as 'self-talk'.

And this talk so easily becomes a self-fulfilling prophecy.

In the habit of feeling bad, we deny ourselves the understanding that making mistakes — and learning from them — is a necessary part of growing and of being alive.

We grow up believing all kind of things about ourselves. And a lot of those things simply aren't true and never were. In fact some of those things are nonsense.

Who says you cannot be a wonderful success? Who says you aren't allowed to speak your mind and have an opinion? Who says you can't stand up in front of groups of people and talk confidently? Who says you can't be calm and confident in social or in work settings? Who says you can't achieve and accomplish whatever you choose to? Who says you don't have the right to be you?

The beliefs that restrict and hold us back were 'programmed' into us when we were too young to realise that they were incorrect and inappropriate.

One helpful way that we can counter negative beliefs is by the simple use of positive affirmations. By using affirmations in a regular, habit-forming way, we weaken and help undo much of the negative programming that we may have experienced.

There are those who say that affirmations just don't work, or that they're counter productive, but my experience is exactly the opposite: they do work. I've used them in my own life and seen them work for countless other people over the years. The key is persistence and repetition.

Habits form because we consistently engage them through simple repetition. And this is the way they are replaced. By forming the habit of meeting negative self-talk with positive affirmations, we eventually replace the automatic negatives with automatic positives. **Positive self-talk is a powerful way of influencing the way we feel about our lives and ourselves.**

Positive self-talk and affirmations don't work their wonders overnight, of course, but then your negative self-talk didn't happen overnight, either.

The good news is that simply by persisting, the change is brought about. And it really doesn't take forever before you begin to experience positive results. So start each day with a positive affirmation. As soon as you wake up, just repeat your chosen affirmation twenty times and then do the same again before sleeping.

Use the affirmation during the day, each time you find yourself engaging in negative self-talk and unhelpful thinking. Stick with it, and the change you want will happen. Start with the first affirmation below. In my opinion it's the most important one:

- *I love and approve of myself*
- *Everything I seek is now seeking me*
- *Each day my life is filled with wonders and magic*

Doesn't sound like much, does it?

Why not try it and see how you get on? If you've tried affirmations before, then this time use them for longer — in fact keep on and on using them. Be patient and don't set a time limit. They really can help you unlock what is already there, inside, just waiting for you to discover and allow: the self you were meant to be — the self you truly are.

**Remember that everything you need you already have.**

After all, to paraphrase that old Chinese saying, why curse the darkness when you have the candle?

*'The purpose of human life is to light a candle
in the darkness of mere existence'*
**Carl Jung**

# It's All in the Perception

S ometimes people who come to me for help in my therapy practice look at me with bewilderment in their eyes when I explain, as I often do, that there really is nothing wrong with them.

Usually that bewilderment fades when they grasp my meaning: The real problem lies not with them, but with their beliefs.

And those beliefs are based on perception. Once the perception is changed then so is the person.

Let me explain.

The simple fact is that, to a large extent, we are our beliefs.

If we believe we are happy, then who is to tell us that we are sad?

If we believe that the world is a bed of thorns, then we will find it difficult to find rest and pain will punctuate our dreams.

So often we see things not as they are, but as our beliefs tell us they are. Practically everything we perceive is filtered through our preexisting beliefs.

But those beliefs themselves had to come from somewhere.

And they came from *perception*.

When we were younger we passed through experiences that were perceived by us in a certain way and so given a particular meaning. The meaning we gave formed our beliefs, our version of reality. We kind of got programmed with it.

In a neat circular symmetry, our perception created our beliefs and now our beliefs influence our perception.

The problem is that our perception was not and is not always in line with the facts.

You see, our perception is the light we shine on the experiences and events in our world. But our perception is very subjective. The world that we experience really depends on where we choose to shine that light and how we choose to shine it.

This is the reason why two different people can pass through very similar experiences with one feeling devastated and the other remaining wholly unaffected and able to get on with life as if little had happened.

For both people the facts are similar, but the perception — and so the meaning — is different.

The really interesting thing is that though we may have limited control over external things, we do have control over the effect those things have upon us because human beings possess the ability to adjust perceptions and amend beliefs.

It is the beliefs we hold — and insist on holding onto — that determine our outlook and our approach to the world and to ourselves. We depend on our beliefs to tell us how things work, what's right and what's wrong, what's important and what's not. Our beliefs tell us what we can expect from situations, from other people, from ourselves and from life in general.

It's just the way we work.

If we are fortunate, then we will have positive beliefs that tell us we are capable, worthwhile, loveable, safe, secure and so on, and that we can expect to go on feeling this way. These beliefs will energise and help us to achieve and accomplish and live a meaningful, satisfying life.

But if we are less fortunate, then we may well harbour unhelpful beliefs that are out of line with reality, and that limit, hold us back, sap our energy and bring us anxiety or pain. With these beliefs we will find life very hard going indeed.

Now, we can hold on to the negative programming of the past, allowing our unhelpful beliefs to dictate our version of reality; we can even nurture grudges, wallow in disappointment, apportion blame and luxuriate in self-pity and guilt. But in doing this we make a choice.

We *choose* to hold ourselves back, working to a script written by someone other than our adult authentic self, a script based entirely on previous interpretations, previous perceptions.

We can do that. Or we can decide to take responsibility for our life and ourselves; we can work on realigning our beliefs and letting go of our negativity. We can *choose* to move forward.

If you are troubled, if your life is feeling like it's stuck and on hold, then perhaps it's time to let go of that way of perceiving, that way of believing.

Let go of the grudges, the resentments, and the limiting beliefs of the past. Let go of the script and you become spontaneous and authentic.

**See yourself as a valuable, loveable, worthwhile, successful person and you begin to move forward**. Do this consistently enough, put in the work and as sure as morning follows night you will become that person — the person you were made to be.

Choose to shine your light wisely and you will see that clarity and joy are what really remain when you let go of those negative beliefs and the perceptions on which they are based.

*'All our knowledge is the offspring of our perceptions'*
**Leonardo da Vinci**

# The Journey

~

L ast month I journeyed to Morocco where I spent some time with the wonderful Berber people in the north.

Though I had visited this beautiful country before, this was the first time I had ventured away from the well-trodden path of cities such as Marrakech and Tangier.

Travelling alone, I was perhaps understandably a little apprehensive when I set out. After all, for me this was largely unmapped territory.

I needn't have worried, of course; though Tunisia, Egypt and Libya had passed through their share of upheaval and unrest, and the turmoil in Syria was about to be unleashed, magical Morocco remained as calm and welcoming as its timeless mosques, its warm and hospitable people and I felt safe as I journeyed on.

Therapy itself has often been compared to a journey and, indeed, I believe it to be a valid metaphor. As a therapist, my job is to guide and walk some of the way with everyone who comes to me for help. Sometimes I go on ahead a little, but most often I take them by the hand and walk by their side.

People who have never been in therapy before are often understandably a little nervous, a little apprehensive as their journey begins, and I do my best to allay their fears, showing them that they are safe and that there really is nothing to fear except perhaps, as Roosevelt so famously pointed out, fear itself.

Those who come to see me have all the courage they need for their voyage into what for them is, I know, largely uncharted territory. As I so often point out, **it's much better to be scared of the journey than it is to close the door.** And in picking up the phone and keeping their appointment they have already gone some way to opening that door.

In therapy windows will need to be cleaned and doors will need to be unlocked and walked through. Some of the people I meet are, at first, afraid of those doors. They seem to have been slammed shut in their face, closed for far too long. But sooner or later most are able to open them and walk through into the better, more positive life that awaits them; the life that was always there just beyond those closed doors.

When the doors have all closed, and the windows become a mirror, do not give up hope. The key is there, somewhere inside, and all you need do is find it.

*'Every day is a journey, and the journey itself is home...'*
**Matsuo Basho**

# The Meaning of Feelings

H ave you ever paused to wonder why we have feelings? If you haven't then you're by no means alone. After all, feelings have been with us in one form or another since before the day we were born and most of us simply take them for granted.

It might not come as a surprise to learn that my work as a hypno-psychotherapist has everything to do with feelings. The great majority of people who come to consult me do so because they are simply not feeling good.

Often those feelings have been there for a very long time, or they may only recently have surfaced. But one thing is sure: they just cannot continue to be ignored.

And that's the thing with feelings: we can only ignore them for so long.

We might attempt to escape our difficult feelings with food, alcohol, drugs or some form of behaviour meant to divert and distract us, but sooner or later our attempts to deny these feelings bring their own difficulties, their own special pain.

When we feel joy, enthusiasm, genuine satisfaction or feelings of inner peace, then we know that we are doing well, that we are probably headed for something great. These feelings tell us that we're doing just fine.

Difficult feelings such as sadness, anger, guilt, frustration, anxiety, fear, or the feelings that come with low self-esteem and lack of confidence are powerful messages being sent from our own subconscious mind in order to inform and help us.

Those difficult feelings tell us that something is wrong; something needs attention.

Instead of attempting to deny or to distract yourself from feelings that you find uncomfortable, pay attention to those feelings. Listen to what they are trying to tell you.

They are not there to control you. They are there to inform and guide you so that you can be the very best you that you can be.

Anger, for example, is there to tell us that we perceive unfairness — someone has been unfair to us or to someone or something we care about. It has a twin: guilt. Guilt is also about unfairness. It tells us that we ourselves have been unfair. Sadness is the feeling that tells us we perceive loss. Frustration is there to let us know that what we are doing just isn't working — try something else.

By understanding what our feelings are trying to tell us we become empowered to do something about them. By attempting to deny and distract ourselves from uncomfortable feelings we make them even more monstrous.

If you are having a difficult journey, if life's road is proving hard and rocky then perhaps it's finally time to listen to what your feelings are really trying to tell you.

No one was born to feel bad. No one was born to live life in a state of frustration or anxiety, fear, worry, anger, guilt or sadness.

Inner peace and the simple joy of being alive really can be yours if you stop denying and attempting to distract yourself from those difficult feelings and finally do something about them.

In your feelings there is great wisdom. **Listen to what they are saying and then take action.**

Yes, it will take work. But it certainly will be worth the effort.

*'If you believe that feeling bad or worrying long enough will change a past or future event, then you are residing on another planet with a different reality system'*
**William James**

# Time to Let Go

~

S o many of the people who come to see me are carrying the past and its hurts with them.

Some are haunted by the mistakes they have made and the hurt that those mistakes have caused.

My response is always the same. It's my job to do all that I can to help people heal, to help them move on — no matter their past.

After all, who amongst us has not made mistakes? Who has lived an entirely selfless and completely blameless life? Who can honestly say that in one way or another they could not have done better?

It's easy to keep on beating yourself up, to go on paying for the past and its wrongs. But what good does that really do? Does that benefit those you have hurt? Does it benefit you?

Whatever your past has been, whatever mistakes or guilt you might still carry with you, you can set it down. Those things you have done or have failed to do you can put behind you now.

You hurt someone? Well, perhaps you did, but haven't you too in some way also been hurt? What point is there now to go on hurting?

If you have lived with regret then you have learned your lesson, and so you have punished yourself enough.

Isn't it time now to forgive yourself and move on?

We cannot re-write the past, but neither can we live there. It was never really meant for that. **If you need to, then start afresh; wipe the slate clean and begin over.** No matter the cost it will be cheaper than remaining in the prison of yesterday.

If you really have learned from what has gone before then let it go now—whatever it is, whatever it was, let it go. The price has been paid, and nobody need again pay for your learning. You can do better from now on and you will not need to make those mistakes again.

Draw that line under yesterday and step over it. There is no need to look back. There was a time to learn, and **now it's time to live**.

> *'In the end these things matter most: How well did you love?*
> *How fully did you love? How deeply did you learn to let go?'*
> **Gautama Buddha**

# Practising Who You Are

~

T he other day I was walking past the Symphony Hall near my Birmingham office when I noticed a young man with a violin case in hand literally running into the building.

Nothing very unusual in this, of course, but it did bring to mind an old story that I heard some years ago. Perhaps you've already heard the story, and I ask your indulgence if you have.

In this particular tale, a young man is hurrying down the street with a violin clutched under his arm. 'Excuse me', he breathlessly asks a passer-by, 'but how do I get to the Symphony Hall?'

'Practise. Practise. Practise', comes the response.

Well, the young man rushing into the Birmingham Symphony Hall obviously had no need of directions. And chances are he'd already done his practice.

Few would deny the value of practice, because we intuitively understand that this is the way we human beings function, the way we operate.

We do indeed do better with practice.

And this is true in so many areas of our life — for good and for bad.

You see, the way in which we learn to play an instrument or train ourselves to be proficient at any new skill — riding a bike or driving a car, for example — is exactly the same way that we practise thoughts and beliefs.

Simple repetition of thoughts and beliefs drives these things deep down where they become a part of us, how we function and feel and how we automatically manifest our reality. What we think we are, what we believe we are, we easily become.

The fact is that each time we tell ourselves we won't be able to do something, each time we tell ourselves that we really aren't worthy or clever or attractive or good enough, then we are practising being that way.

We are setting things up and teaching ourselves how to become these things.

It's the combination of a couple of simple laws — the Law of Expectation — what the mind expects to happen tends to be realised, and the Law of Focus — what you say to yourself, about yourself, you tend to become.

The mind is structured in such a way that it will expect whatever we program it to expect — and it does its very best to deliver on this.

Yet just as we practise doubt and failure and low self-esteem, just as we set ourselves up to become these things, we could as easily practise being successful. We could be programming ourselves to be positive, healthy and optimistic. It's simply a question of directing our internal resources in a helpful and self-validating manner.

Maybe **now is the time to allow yourself to practise being what you really can be** — that positive, life-affirming self that you know, deep down, you really are.

Perhaps now is the time to tap into your own inner power and allow yourself to discover how good it really does feel to be you.

*'There is neither beginning to practise, nor end to enlightenment.*
*There is no beginning to enlightenment, nor end to practise'*
**Dogen (1200 - 1253)**

# Borrowed Dreams

~

The woman seated opposite me looked so very sad. 'Sometimes I feel as if it's all one great big dream', she said, and she reached over and sipped her tea.

'We can all have that feeling from time to time', I reassured her.

'Yes', she said, 'but the problem is I don't know whether the dream is mine or someone else's…'

'Well, then, let's find out, shall we?' And we set about our work together.

So many of the people who come to see me in my role as a therapist have a similar difficulty, though not everyone is able to express it as this woman did.

Like her they have drifted into someone else's dream, someone else's idea of what to do, where to live, how to enjoy the only life they will ever really have. But living in this way is to live on borrowed dreams. And borrowed dreams can only last for so long before they must be given back.

**The life we desire and the life we deserve will never come from following someone else's dream, or someone else's idea of what our life should be.**

It is only when we have the courage to dream our own dreams, follow our own path, that we can truly live the life that has been gifted to us. **You have the courage.** It's there inside you waiting for you to use. You have been given the life. That's there too, and it's there in abundance, but it won't be there forever.

It's up to you to dream your dreams. It's up to you to live your life.

*'Who looks without dreams;*
*who looks within awakens…'*
**Carl Jung**

# The Freedom to Fall

～

One of the beauties of modern technology is the freedom that it can afford us. Today I am taking advantage of that freedom; it is a sun-filled Sunday and I am writing this month's column on my little laptop on a bench in my local park.

Around me are the young and the old, friends, lovers, families. The sun is smiling and children are playing. One little girl has just fallen and grazed her knee. She is crying and mum is there soothing and comforting. Soon she will get back into the swing of things and that little fall will be all but forgotten.

Why is it that children are able to make such wonderful progress, to move with such apparent rapidity from being helpless babies to becoming capable young people?

Well, one of the reasons is that they are not so very afraid of making mistakes. They simply learn as they go, naturally developing the most complex of abilities, from the motor skills required in order to balance, to the intricacies of language patterns and communication.

Despite this little girl's tears, she cares much less about falling. Children stumble and fall, they make mistakes and through these things they naturally progress, they learn and they grow.

As adults we have a tendency to be a bit more protective of our mistakes. We just don't like to make them, or to admit them, and so we spend so much of our time and energy in trying to avoid them.

Yet the simple truth is that **when we focus only on avoiding mistakes we set ourselves up to avoid achievement**. By allowing ourselves to be consistently worried about getting it wrong, we can so easily prevent ourselves from getting it right.

Life really does want us to succeed. It does everything needed in order that we do this. It gives us the learnings and the means to access those learnings and, yes, that means that sometimes life's teachings will come in the guise of the mistakes we make.

One thing is certain: we will make mistakes, we will stumble and sometimes we will fall. But in so doing we will also live, because inherent in those mistakes and falls is the learning each one of us needs in order to move forward with our life.

In getting it wrong we somehow learn how to get it right.

Each time you stumble, learn the lesson — and then get back up again.

**Be grateful for the learning**; see it as an opportunity to grow and to make life better and before you know it you will find yourself stumbling no more.

*'The only real mistake is the one from which we learn nothing'*
**John Powell**

# Time to Stop Running

∽

As a working hypno-psychotherapist, I regularly meet and talk with people who have spent year after year wrestling with the same old problem.

Some have tried prescription medication, alcohol, drugs, geographic relocation and a whole range of various alternative means in a vain attempt to escape the difficulties that have troubled them for so very long.

Most have tried denying and distracting themselves from the awkward feelings that have caused them so much anxiety, worry and upset.

Many have spent years trying to avoid those situations and experiences that might potentially provoke feelings of fear, embarrassment or discomfort.

Yet such strategies seem to have brought them little, if any success. Often it is the behaviour that people have adopted in order to try to distract or deal with those difficult feelings that has become a problem in and of itself.

By the time they arrive in my office, most people have reached the point where they can no longer avoid; they can no longer continue to live a life full of denial.

So often I hear the plaintive cry: 'You are my last hope'.

'Then are you ready at last to do whatever you need to do in order to change?' I ask. Only when the answer is 'Yes!' are they truly ready. They have finally come to that place where they really can be helped.

Why is this? Well, it's because only when a person is able to bring forth the inner honesty that says: 'I am ready to stop avoiding, resisting and rationalizing and finally *do* something about my problem' that he or she can allow real and lasting change to take place.

Only by ending the denial and the resistance can we let go of the limitations and blockages that have held us back and prevented us from achieving the balance and personal freedom that is each person's birthright.

The reality is that problems just do not dissolve and disappear simply through denial and distraction.

That great psychologist Carl Jung knew exactly what he was talking about when he said that 'all human neurosis is a substitute for legitimate suffering'.

No amount of medication meant to soften the symptoms and no behaviour intended to distract us from our difficulties will ever work for very long. Sooner or later, our problems must be addressed and worked through or they will remain forever an obstacle and a hindrance, a straightjacket from which we have no real chance of escaping.

Perhaps now is the time to become honest. Perhaps now is the time to stop running away and to ask yourself the real nature of what you have been avoiding and fleeing from. When you're open to this, then you are in a wonderful position to do something about it.

After all, isn't it better to face it, to deal with it now, rather than to continue as you have been, wasting so many precious hours, days and years bound up with anxiety, fear and discomfort?

**The way out is to do something about it.** If this means reaching out and asking for help, then this is what needs to be done.

Why continue to waste all that effort in denial? You could just as easily do something about what has been bothering you.

Think of how good it will be once you are free to be yourself.

This is your life. Treat it as the only one you have and make sure that you do not waste it.

*'You cannot run away from yourself.*
*When you do you're right behind you'*
**Fortune Cookie**

# Today

~

Today is your chance to start again. Yesterday, with its troubles and its triumphs has gone now, and its slate can be wiped clean. There's no need to linger there. Let it go now and move on.

Why allow regret to spoil the opportunity that this day now brings? The mistakes you made have given you more wisdom, because you have a much better idea now of what works and what fails to work.

Put that wisdom to work for you now. Today you are more experienced and that means that you're better prepared than ever before.

**Today you can pull out all the stops and move forward.** There's no need to wait any longer. Take that step, put one foot in front of the other and move on with your life. It's the only one you have, and if you live it then it's the only one you'll ever need.

Today you can push beyond the fear, find the courage... reach beyond yourself. Today you can surprise yourself by really starting to live at last.

Whether or not it is clear to you, you are here for a reason. Against so many odds your life has brought you to this new day, this new chance. Reach out and take it now.

**Inside you there is a light that can illuminate your way.** And all you need do is to let it shine today.

There really is nothing to stop you. Go ahead now, live today.

It will never come again.

*'Live as you would have wished to have lived*
*when you are dying'*
**Christian Fürchtegott Gellert**

# Focus

One of the many wonderful things that people can do in hypnosis is to learn how to let go of the endless distractions that surround us and really focus.

In fact, the ability to constructively use hypnosis in this way is an aspect that many successful people — from sporting greats like Tiger Woods and celebrated actors like Matt Damon, to brilliant minds like Albert Einstein and Henry Ford — have taken full advantage of.

The inventor of that first Ford motor car, Henry Ford, for example, himself a great believer in hypnosis, used the trance state in order to access his own innate imagination, to focus in on his own inner creativity. Through the use of hypnosis he vastly increased his understanding of the nature of the subconscious mind and the power of the beliefs that became established there.

It was this understanding that helped him to break the mould of that which had gone before, allowing him to change not only his own reality, but the reality of countless generations that came after him through the process of mass production.

Through hypnosis he came to see that it is our focus on the beliefs we hold — and hold onto — that really determines the life we live, the reality we inhabit.

It was Ford who famously said: 'Whether you think you can, or you think you can't — you're right!' and it was Einstein who used dream and trance states in order to facilitate and develop his ideas, he who said: 'Imagination is more important than knowledge'.

Imagination, of course, is the very language of the subconscious mind, just as logic is the language of the conscious mind. In hypnosis we access the subconscious, imaginative mind directly.

With hypnosis Henry Ford, Albert Einstein, Tiger Woods, Matt Damon and countless others learned how to 'enter the zone', reducing or eliminating outside distractions and bringing about a state of real focus, a state in which their own talents and inner wisdom might simply spring forth.

Hypnosis helped them to focus on the things that mattered most and consequently, to bring those things into reality. Of course, we do not need to be in the trance state of hypnosis in order to focus.

But we do need to realise that the things we focus on have a real tendency to become the reality that we live.

If we focus on resentment, for example, then we simply create more things to resent. When we focus on anger, then we will go right on finding other things about which to become angry.

If, on the other hand, we focus on an attitude of gratitude for life's abundance, then we will bring so many things into our life and into our reality, things for which we can be truly grateful.

**Focus on what you can give and you will increase those things that you can have.**

In choosing our focus we can choose the very direction of our own life, because the simple truth is that where our focus lies, there our life is headed.

And the wonderful thing is that we really can choose what to focus upon. Yes, it might take some practice and yes, it is probably easier to do this systematically in the trance state of hypnosis, but we do not need to be in a hypnotic state in order to accomplish this.

**With regular practice and persistence we can learn to make a habit of it at any time.**

By consistently choosing where your focus lies, you can alter your perception, choose your reality and change your life.

After all, all it really takes is a simple change of focus.

*'The successful person is the average person, focused'*
**Anonymous**

# Whole Again

⁓

There are times in life when all we really need to feel better is to let go. And nowhere is this truer than with the past.

But letting go of the past is not always the easiest thing to do.

Each one of us has a past, and in that past, along with the joy and the laughter, we will have gone through experiences that were sometimes unfair or unjust.

When we experience unfairness there are really only two basic emotions that we can feel, and these are anger and guilt. Anger is the name of the emotion we feel when we think that someone else has been unfair, and guilt is the feeling we encounter when we believe that it is we, ourselves, who have acted unfairly.

Both of these emotions exist for a reason. They are meant to inform and to instruct, and then to be released and let go.

The problem is that all too often these powerful feelings can become internalised, as if they are a part of us. We carry them within, sometimes for years, and all they do is to weigh us down, hold us back and stop us from being the person we were meant to be.

No matter the form or the origin of the unfairness, whether visited upon or created by us, there has to come a time when we move on with our lives, letting go of the past.

And so often this means that we need to forgive.

It really does not matter whether the person who has offended us deserves or merits our forgiveness. That is not the point. By hanging onto our anger it is we ourselves who continue to be hurt and held back.

**Once we have learned guilt's lesson then we are unlikely to repeat it** and it serves no useful purpose to continue punishing ourselves with this painful emotion.

Now is the time to draw that line under the past and move on.

Now is the time to forgive, and to once more become whole.

> *'Forgiveness is the answer to the child's dream of a miracle*
> *by which what is broken is made whole again,*
> *what is soiled is made clean again...'*
> **Dag Hammarskjold**

# Free to Be

$\sim$

S o often clients come to me and tell me how unfairly life has been treating them. Often and understandably they blame their partner, their family, or their past for their present troubles and difficulties.

Yet when I ask them the simple question:

'Is there anyone in your life whom you treat as badly as you treat yourself?' No one has ever answered in the affirmative. No one has ever said, 'yes'.

This is the paradox: So very often we blame others for our woes and yet we would never dream of treating others in the way that we treat ourselves.

You know, there was a time before we saw others as the source of our own sadness and joy. It may well have been a very long time ago, but this, I believe, is our natural state of being.

It is we and we alone who determine what really affects us. And while it is true that external facts play their part, it is in the response we give to these facts that joy and sorrow truly exist. In reality, it is we who choose the degree to which we are affected by the experiences through which we pass.

Sooner or later we need to accept the simple truth that it is we ourselves who decide our happiness and our sadness.

If my work as a therapist has taught me one thing, it is that it is the perception — the interpretation of our experiences — and what we do with that perception, which is so very much more powerful than the facts, the experiences themselves.

Yes, we can blame others and depend on others and believe that the world would end without that special person in it. We can wait a whole lifetime for that knight in shining armour or that fairy godmother to come and save us from ourselves or to give our life a meaning and a purpose.

If we are fortunate we can share our journey with another, we can form unions, alliances and partnerships. We can travel part of the road with others, but they cannot come with us all of the way. They cannot come with us to where we are going, nor can we go with them.

We are going to die.

Those who care for and about us may accompany us to the gates of death, but it is we alone who must pass through those gates and enter into that mystery.

Surely there is a lesson in this. And I believe that lesson has something to do with personal responsibility.

I believe that we can and should live our lives in a kind, caring and compassionate way, an aware and a responsible way. But we can only do this if we are kind, caring and compassionate towards ourselves too.

The true lesson that death holds for each one of us is that, first and foremost, we need to become responsible for ourselves.

When we become aware, truly aware, that this moment holds all the joy and all the sadness that we allow, then we become free to live this moment.

We become free to live our lives in the knowledge, and not in the fear, of death. **We become free to be.**

> *'What the caterpillar calls the end*
> *the rest of the world calls a butterfly'*
> **Lao-Tzu**

# When the Weeds Take Over the Garden

∽

R ecently, I was helping a friend who had been going through a bit of a rough spell.

He had been in hospital and so had left his garden untended for a while and the weeds had lost no time in flourishing.

So there I was, stooping and bending, and in my own very small way tilling the earth. At the end of the day, my back naturally felt a little sore, but in a strange way, merely pulling up those weeds had refreshed and lifted my spirit.

Perhaps it was the simple act of re-connecting with the earth, or maybe it was the feeling of satisfaction that comes from having taken a step, small though it may have been, in helping a friend to put things in order.

For the Anglo Saxons, August was *Weod Monoth* — weed month — because they saw it as the month in which weeds grew most rapidly.

In August and in every other month, clients often come to me with the feeling that the weeds have taken over the garden. They feel stuck and unable to move forward and are looking for a way to grow and to get on with their life.

They are, quite simply, ready for change.

Yet **in order for things to change, we need to change**. And that is something that each one of us has to take personal responsibility for.

Until this readiness and the willingness to take personal responsibility for change is there, very little can be accomplished.

Indeed, part of my job as a therapist consists in helping people to understand that while psychotherapy and hypnosis can most certainly help and rapidly accelerate the process of change; neither it nor I can change *for* them.

After all, if your feet hurt, what good is it to you if I change my shoes?

No, real change is something that happens within the individual. It is something that cannot be done to or for someone. It can only take place when the person is prepared to take responsibility for that change.

It's easy to feel stuck… in one way or another, we've all been there.

But there really is no need to remain stuck, **challenging and scary though change may sometimes appear**.

We know that life is full of challenge. It's what keeps us moving forward and growing. Can you imagine a life without any kind of challenge?

How boring and unproductive that life would be!

Yet we know too that challenge can produce many different feelings, from elation to disappointment. And it's often the feelings of disappointment that fool us into thinking we are stuck, leaving us feeling unable, or afraid, to move on.

If you are feeling stuck, with too many weeds in your garden, then there really is something you can do about it.

No matter how much life has seemed to disappoint you, no matter how much you may feel that you have disappointed yourself, you can move forward. And the only way to do this is to take that first step.

Now, here is the thing: You can take that step in any direction you like, but you need to do it from where you are. And there really is no better time to start than now.

As the sage once said: 'The tragedy of life is not that it is too short, but that we wait too long to begin it'.

Why wait any longer? **If you are truly ready for change, why not take that first step today?**

Be the change, and your spirit will surely reward you.

*'What you will be is what you do now'*
**Gautama Buddha**

# Weather, Ducks and Us

〜

It's really miserable weather out there', said my client as she seated herself in the chair opposite me.

I turned around to look briefly out of the window at the grey sky and the red brick buildings beyond, and as I did so I glanced down to where a family of ducks were happily paddling their way single file along the canal.

'Well', I said, 'it certainly does look a bit grey, but come and look at what I can see', and as I pointed to the ducks, a little smile passed involuntarily across her face.

'Perhaps it's only we who are miserable', I said, 'not the weather', and we got down to the reason for her visit.

So much of what we see, what we perceive, is observed through the lens of our own particular attitude towards life. Practically everything we experience is filtered through this.

The world that surrounds us is simply a reflection of the world that is within us, and not the other way around, no matter what rationalisations we might make to the contrary.

If you have been blaming the weather, or your past, or your current situation for the way you have been feeling then isn't it time you did something about it?

You are not powerless. You have the ability to alter the way you see, the way you perceive, the way you feel. **You have the ability to change the way you live.**

Look objectively at the beliefs that are holding you back and making you feel as you do and ask yourself if those beliefs really are justified, or if they, too, were the product of a faulty way of seeing.

Then take action. Begin to work on those beliefs. Systematically examine them and see them for what they really are. Begin to replace them with more positive, life-affirming beliefs, ones that will help you move forward.

When we let go of our limiting beliefs then we let go of our limiting expectations, our limiting interpretations of life itself.

**You were born to shine.**

It may be grey outside, but with the right attitude you can be as spritely as a duck in water.

*'If I have the belief that I can do it, I shall surely acquire the capacity to do it even if I may not have it at the beginning'*
**Mahatma Gandhi**

# Change

∽

The life we are living is the result of all we have done so far. Each experience we have passed through has had its effect on us, but it is we who choose what to hold onto and what to let go of.

If it is true that we live our life as a tale that is told, then it is we ourselves who write the story.

Understanding this is the key to change.

We can choose to act as if there is no choice, as if our life and everything in it is already written in stone, immutable and unchangeable. But if we live in this way, then we become somehow less than human, we become helpless cogs in a clockwork machine, smaller and more insignificant, prey to whatever does the winding.

We can live in this way, and many people do.

Or we can choose to act as if we really do have a choice, as if we are not merely helpless puppets whose strings are pulled by fate, or by the past, or by other people. **Being the author of our own fate, we can alter the plot, amend the script, and change the ending.**

After all, this is *our* story, and we its writer.

If we are not happy with our story, if we want our story to change then we too must be willing to change. This means taking responsibility for ourselves. There really is no other way.

Simply dreaming of a better, easier life will not bring it into being. If you truly want your life to change, then you will need to leave whatever comfortable trance you've been reclining in and do something different.

It may mean you'll need to change your work, your friends, the dynamic of your relationships, the foods you eat or where you live. It will probably take courage, but if you've made it this far, then you have already dealt with change and **you have courage enough**.

Don't let fear hold you back. Look your fear in the face and push on anyway. Go forward. Do this once and your confidence, your self-esteem, changes for the better. Keep right on doing this and so does the story of your life.

**Whether you like it or not, change will happen.** You can choose to be the victim of that change or you can choose to be its author.

The choice really is yours.

*'Because things are the way they are,*
*things will not stay the way they are'*
**Bertolt Brecht**

# Understanding

~

A couple of weekends ago I found myself leafing through an old, dog-eared set of *Encyclopaedia Britannica* at a car boot sale.

As a younger man, it was my dream to own a complete set of this remarkable compendium of human knowledge and erudition. In those far off salad days, the *Britannica* seemed to me to be the embodiment of knowledge and information.

Time passed and, years later, I was fortunate enough to be able to buy my own set and it became a wonderful source of information, knowledge and joy.

Yet knowledge — unlike understanding — can so very quickly become out of date and before very long even the updating yearbooks couldn't keep up with the rapidly changing world.

As I prized my mind out of the 20th and into the 21st Century, the 'information highway' of the Internet replaced my encyclopaedia.

A simple entry into Google or any search engine would give me as much information on just about any subject as I could possibly want or even desire.

I still continue to read books, of course, but neither they nor the Internet can think for me.

You see, long before I made that jump to the Internet, I had learned something of real importance: **Knowledge and information are valuable and worthwhile, but it is understanding that is truly rare and precious.**

Today our world is awash with information. Yet information without understanding is the stuff of which monsters are made.

The fact is that information tells us something of what has happened and something of what is happening. Understanding allows us a clearer picture of what will come as a result of this.

**Understanding gives us vision.** It allows us to see possibilities that others cannot even glimpse.

The time and effort we put into understanding brings real value to our life and to our world.

And nowhere is this truer than in the journey of self-understanding.

If you are stuck, lost, troubled or confused, ask yourself this: Is the information that you have built your views and opinions upon still true and relevant? Is it really current and correct?

Or is the opinion you have of yourself, of your abilities and of your expectations — of your own future and your own world — simply based on information 'programmed' into you at some time in your past?

Have the courage to break free of your past, of your received opinions and beliefs. Seek not simply to know, but also to understand.

Do this and you will begin to live a wisdom that no book or search engine can ever provide.

More than this, you will become authentically you.

*'I do not want the peace that passeth understanding.*
*I want the understanding which bringeth peace'*
**Helen Keller**

SEPTEMBER
*Week Four*

# Belonging to Tomorrow, Missing Today

~

W ho among us has not put off until tomorrow what we should have done today — only to find that when tomorrow came our thinking was still: 'Well, there's always tomorrow...'?

As far as procrastination is concerned, tomorrow seems to play an extraordinarily important part in our lives. According to the *Oxford Dictionary*, the very origins of the word procrastination mean 'belonging to tomorrow'.

Odd considering all we ever really have is today.

There seems to be no getting away from it, procrastination is just part of the human condition, something we all engage in from time to time.

It's nothing to become overly concerned about, of course; in fact, a little procrastination may even serve a useful purpose, affording us a welcome break or breather. But then, we soon get back in there, taking care of those things that really do need our attention.

Yet with chronic procrastination, this simply isn't the case. Indeed, it can turn us into our own worst enemy.

When procrastination becomes a real issue is when it consistently prevents us from doing what really does need to be done and done now.

If we were to ask most people exactly why they procrastinate, we'd very likely get a whole catalogue of familiar excuses: 'I need to be in the right mood'; 'There's still time'; 'I work better under pressure'; and on and on.

85

What we're less likely to get is the truth.

Because the truth is that, most often, we have no clear idea why we procrastinate. We just seem to find ourselves caught in a web of delay and postponement, putting off things and missing opportunities.

And all the time the pressure builds until frustration and self-disappointment set in, which just complicates and compounds things, maybe even adding an element of guilt that makes us feel even worse.

If this sounds all too familiar to you, then read on, but be prepared for some adjustments in your thinking, because I'm going to list some of the real reasons people procrastinate, as determined by researchers at Ohio State University.

As you read, it might be worth noticing just how many of these real reasons have to do with emotions and with self-belief.

- *Perfectionism* — When we equate performance with self-worth, procrastination seems to offer protection from failure. 'If I don't start, I can't fail.'
- *Need for Love* — When we feel others will only accept us if we perform well, procrastination seems to protect us from rejection. 'If I don't begin, I cannot be rejected.'
- *Anticipating the Worst* — When we can only imagine disaster as the outcome of our activity, then procrastination seems to protect us from anxiety. 'If I delay, then I might avoid catastrophe.'
- *Self-Judgement* — When we judge ourselves too harshly, procrastination seems to offer protection from feelings of self-hate and shame. 'If I don't begin, then I can't beat myself up.'
- *Depression* — When we feel overwhelmed, then procrastination appears to protect us from feelings of helplessness. 'If I don't make a start, then I won't sink.'
- *Rigid Identity* — When our image of our self is set in concrete, then procrastination protects us from having to change. 'If I don't begin, then I can remain as I am.'

Some pretty hard truths, right? Did you notice how many of these things have to do with feelings of self-worth and self-esteem?

Now, here's the essential understanding: the base and repository of self-belief is the subconscious mind. It's here that both self-limiting — as well as self-empowering — beliefs are maintained and stored.

It's in the subconscious mind that beliefs are most powerful, functioning and running just like programs in a computer, driving outcomes, powerfully affecting our actions or, in the case of procrastination, our lack of action.

Yes, there are a good number of things you can do in order to cope with procrastination, but until the basic, underlying reasons for endless postponement are uncovered and neutralised, then procrastination will continue to rear its slothful head again and again.

And, so often, this involves a re-alignment of our internal self-image, our sense of self-worth.

In terms of frustration, lack of personal growth and advancement, a 'putting off until tomorrow' attitude really can damage and hold us back. Yet as with so many other areas in life, we begin to make a difference just as soon as we allow ourselves to take that first step towards change.

After all, if today is all we ever really have, what sense is there in fooling ourselves that we belong to tomorrow?

You have it in you to take that first step today.

Why not start now?

> *'You don't have to see the whole staircase,*
> *just take the first step'*
> **Martin Luther King, Jr.**

# Accomplishment

W ell, it's October. Once more, the summer is behind us and again the seasons are changing.

We may have started the month with rain or beautiful warm weather, the Indian summer of myth, but all too soon the brief sun-filled gaiety of summer, like our longed-for holidays, must give way to change.

Left, for the fortunate, are the memories that will stay with us through the reflective autumn days and long into the winter.

Summers and holidays come and go, just as they need to. After all, even pleasure can become monotonous. The things that last seem all to be built on accomplishment.

Though we may not always be aware of it, we are given such clear choices. We can continue to repeat each day, idling away our time on Earth, or we can use each precious day, appreciate each fresh new gift of life.

Every day we live we will have things to do, but what we do is not necessarily what we are getting done, what we are really accomplishing.

**Accomplishment is the cornerstone of satisfaction, respect and confidence.** It comes in many forms, but every one of those forms requires passion.

For some, accomplishment is all about material accumulation, social status and influence, but attractive as these things may be for many, they can all be lost and taken from us in an instant.

For others, accomplishment has a different, broader sense, a sense that encompasses personal growth and a greater awareness of life's rich gifts.

When we invest in this kind of accomplishment we are nurtured and nourished through all of our seasons. This kind of accomplishment lets us see the beauty of nature and the wonder of existence; it gives us an appreciation of friendship, and of the lasting power of love.

The world in which we live has its material dimension. We need to take care of the bills and the holidays. This is all well and good, as long as the things we strive for and acquire don't end up owning us.

But if we really want to live a balanced life then we need to be passionate about it; we need to appreciate and work on accomplishing those things that cannot fade.

These are the things that will last long after the seasons have ended, long after the days are gone.

*'Every great accomplishment is the story of a flaming heart...'*
**Arnold H. Glasgow**

# Born to Win

⚬

Not so long ago an acquaintance of mine related an experience from his childhood.

As a young boy his teacher had asked the class what they wanted to do when they left school and the boy had innocently answered that he would like to become a pilot.

'You? A pilot?' retorted the teacher, 'they don't even let people like you wash airplanes, let alone pilot them!'

As the man spoke his eyes reddened as if fighting back tears. This was more than forty years later; almost half a century had passed and still the experience haunted him.

He never did become a pilot. Though intelligent, for years he struggled in the most menial of jobs. For years he plodded along following the script written for him by people like his teacher.

That script that said he was worthless and incapable of ever becoming anything of value.

He believed what his teacher had told him and that belief determined his reality.

Each day I meet people just like that man. They, too, have bought into someone else's script; they too have accepted faulty beliefs about whom and what they are and what they can expect from life.

Often the script that they have been acting out was written long ago, in childhood.

Before the age of six or seven we are all in a state of trance. We simply have not had the time to develop a sufficient database that would allow us to analyse and compare, to filter the perceptions being fed from the outside world. So we accept beliefs unquestioningly, even when those beliefs are false.

And because we are, to such a large extent, our beliefs, those beliefs determine our reality. Simply put, our beliefs become the life that we live.

The good news is that you can change your beliefs. And in so doing, you can change your life.

Stop for just a moment and consider your hopes, your aspirations and your dreams. They are yours for a reason, yet they are not carved in stone.

Now ask yourself this: **Are you selling yourself short because of your beliefs? Are your beliefs helping you or holding you back?**

There is no divine law that compels you to feel shy or fearful, insufficient or inadequate. No power on earth can force you to live a life of quiet desperation or to be a failure if you truly choose otherwise.

The truth is that you were born to live this life to the full. As much as the trees, and the birds that sing from those trees, you have a right to be here and to enjoy your time while you are here.

**The race is not won at the starting line, nor is it finished there.** Whatever experiences you have passed through, those experiences are not you. They never were you.

It really isn't too late.

You were born to shine and to be a winner. Your winning does not mean that someone else must lose. Life is abundant enough. Each and every one of us can be a winner.

It is the beliefs you hold — and hold onto — that really determine success or failure. And your beliefs *can* be changed. You can change them and in so doing you can change your life.

What's stopping you now?

*'It's never too late to be what you might have been'*
**George Eliot**

# It's Not Too Late

⁓

L ast weekend I did something I had never done before; I went sailing.

I must admit that I had hesitated to take my friend up on the offer so late in the season. Wouldn't it be better to wait until next year, in the summer? Haven't we left it a bit too late now?

Fortunately my friend, an old salt if ever there was one, was having none of it. 'Of course it's not too late!' he insisted and so off we went down to the sea.

He was right, of course. It really wasn't too late and though it was only a small two man dinghy, how I enjoyed the experience! With the wind in my hair and the salt spray on my lips I hung over the side, loving every moment of it, filled with the joy of being alive.

Later, as I was attempting to make the adjustment to walking on dry land I turned to my sailing partner, who incidentally is a psychologist, and heard myself saying: 'I wish I'd done this years ago!' And we both broke out laughing.

So often in my clinical practice I hear those words: 'I wish I'd done this years ago!'

My response is always more or less the same: 'Well, now you have done it and now the rest of your life is yours to live. Go ahead and make every moment count!'

This feeling that it really is too late; that we've missed the boat, is a terrible, disempowering feeling, but it's one that many of us have felt in one way or another at some time on our life's journey.

The mistake we make, of course, is in believing that there's only one boat. But this is hardly ever true. On life's ocean there are many boats, many ships, though we may not always see them coming on the horizon. If we simply wait around like we have been shipwrecked, giving up hope and believing that nothing can change now, then that is the life we will live, the reality that we will get.

With this attitude, our ship will never come in.

Whatever has happened or failed to happen in your life, whatever you have had to live with or are still struggling with, whatever your fear, it is not who you are. It never was.

**There is still time to live your life**, still time to be you — and that time can begin now.

Joy, satisfaction and an inner peace are yours if you will only reach out and claim them.

After all, what better time is there than now?

*'The best time to plant a tree is twenty years ago.*
*The second best time is now'*
**Chinese Proverb**

# An Attitude of Gratitude

⌒

L ast month I travelled to Poland in order to visit Auschwitz and Birkenau concentration camps. It was a journey I had long delayed and, as I had anticipated, it was amongst the most moving and humbling experiences of my life.

It is impossible to visit these sites — the electric fences and barbed wire; the mountains of human hair, shoes, spectacles; the brutal deprivation and torture cells; the gas chamber and crematorium; the wall after wall full of photographs documenting just a fraction of those human beings whose lives were so appallingly stolen from them — without feeling a terrible sense of melancholy, awe and humility.

The incomprehensible brutality and suffering for which these death camps are infamous leaves us with such a deep sadness. That we are capable of doing *these* things fills one with such profound disappointment. Yet it puts things so keenly into perspective, forcing us to recognise that whatever our own troubles might be, they really are quite insignificant compared to what they might have been.

And with this realisation, mingling in with the shock and the horror comes a feeling of intense, almost overwhelming gratitude for what we have and how lucky we truly are to have it.

So often we take our lives and everything in our lives for granted. So often we are blind to the wonderful abundance, which not only surrounds each one of us, but is within each one of us.

In his book *Man's Search for Meaning*, Auschwitz survivor and psychiatrist Viktor Frankl records how misery, deprivation and suffering made even the smallest and most mundane of things truly important and meaningful.

'The spirit reached out for them longingly', he observes.

Surrounded by starvation, deprivation, appalling cruelty and inhumanity, prisoners' minds became focused on that which they once took for granted and did not appreciate.

'In my mind I took bus rides, unlocked the front door of my apartment, answered my telephone, switched on the electric lights. Our thoughts often centred on such details, and these memories could move one to tears', writes Frankl.

In the midst of horror and ugliness, even the smallest, most mundane of experiences could take on real significance.

The simple recognition of beauty, when seeing the magnificent, glowing sky reflected in a muddy puddle was enough to bring a hushed reverence to those prisoners who noticed it. As Frankl reports: 'Then, after minutes of moving silence, one prisoner said to another: "How beautiful the world could be".'

Never was a truer word ever spoken. That we are capable of seeing *these* things fills one with such wonderful hope.

With all its pain and heartbreak, its difficulties and disappointments, the world — our world — really can be beautiful. It is here, waiting for us to recognise this, allow this.

We are gifted with life for such a brief time. And in life, mixed right in with the difficulties and disappointments there is tremendous joy. Yes, perhaps that joy is sometimes difficult to feel. But on other days, and at other times, that joy can simply be palpable, almost tangible. No matter how much or how little we are aware of it, joy is always unfailingly there awaiting us.

And all we need do is to wake up to this simple truth.

There really is no need to wait until we are ill in order to appreciate health, no need to wait until we are alone in order to appreciate friendship, no need to wait until we are homeless in order to appreciate that we are warm and dry and have a roof over our head: No need to be on our death bed in order to appreciate life.

We can start right now. And all it takes is a genuine willingness to foster an 'attitude of gratitude'.

Because the fact is that we can and we do choose our own attitude, towards ourselves and towards life. And attitudes can be re-framed and re-aligned. They can be changed.

Everything we need is right here, inside us, waiting for us to awaken to.

It's not there in some of us; it's in each and every one of us. And it's there now.

Choose to live your life in a positive 'attitude of gratitude' and your whole existence becomes somehow different. Rejoice in even the smallest of things and observe how your life becomes transformed.

Unlike those souls interred in the blasphemy of Auschwitz and Birkenau, we are lucky, we have a choice. 'How beautiful the world could be...' And all we have to do is change could to can, and to allow it. We don't need to be victims. It really is within our power to change things.

You don't even need to let life come to you. It is already here. Learn to welcome every bit of it, with all its wonders and all its shortcomings.

**Learn to be grateful for it.**

What are you waiting for?

You really can start — right now!

*'How wonderful it is that nobody need wait a single moment before starting to improve the world'*
**Anne Frank**

# Another Look at Forgiveness

~

Does it sometimes feel as if you're carrying the whole world on your shoulders? Would you like to lighten the load?

Then maybe it's time you took another look at forgiveness. If you've struggled with it before, it just might be that you're ready for it now.

Few things weigh us down more than anger that has passed its use-by date or guilt that has outlasted its usefulness.

OK, perhaps you've had some tough breaks. Perhaps someone has been downright unfair to you. Perhaps you've been hurt and are still carrying that hurt around inside. Maybe you've hurt someone else and are still suffering because of it. But there is a way to get out from under that burden.

You do have a choice. There is a key that will unlock those chains and set you free... That key is forgiveness.

Yes, we can go on playing the blame game. We can continue to blame others or ourselves for the unfair things that have happened. But where does that really get us?

In continuing to blame others for our troubles we remain their victim. In continuing to blame ourselves we remain stuck in the past.

You can continue in your belief that you just cannot change, or that it's not your fault or your responsibility, but that will only confirm your role as victim or martyr, and all this will accomplish is more regret, as even more of your life ebbs away. But it doesn't have to be this way.

**As long as you live you have choices.**

No matter what has happened, no matter what the past or anyone in it has done to you, it is yours now. It belongs to you. And once you own something then you can do whatever you like with it. And that includes letting it go.

Perhaps those who have hurt you do not deserve the release that forgiveness brings — but you do. In failing to forgive we remain in chains; we go on hurting.

Forgiveness does not mean that we forget, it does not mean that we condone what has happened, it does not mean that we have to love or even like the person that has hurt us.

It does mean that we change. **When we forgive we free ourselves of the past**, our load is lightened and our future automatically becomes brighter.

Isn't it time to lighten your load and move on with your life now?

If you are carrying anger or guilt or any other burden from the past then you can put your load down and start afresh. Find a way to forgive, choose to forgive, and you will do just that.

*'Without forgiveness there is no future...'*
**Desmond Tutu**

# The Courage to Be Happy

～

As a working therapist I am well aware that it takes courage to reach out and ask for help.

Often people tell me that they have been thinking about coming to see me for months. Sometimes they have returned to my website time and again telling themselves that they really should get in touch and begin the process of change.

In fact, each new client who walks into my office has done so because they found the courage to take that first step.

And because they have taken that first step towards change, then I know we can build on that courage. I know that they have all the courage they need in order to confront their fears and to grow.

They have the courage to change.

And so do you.

With or without a therapist you can begin the process of change, but this can only happen once you face your problems.

We know that every life has its share of difficulty and discomfort.

But we can only stick our head in the sand and hide away for so long. Sooner or later we have no alternative but to confront and tackle the cause of our difficulties.

Trying to avoid these things simply makes them worse. It deepens and entrenches the problem and increases the difficulty when you're finally left with no choice but to tackle it.

**The sooner you get started the less there will be to confront.**

You have it within you to choose to address your fears now instead of waiting for them to grow stronger. Ask yourself: Would you rather deal with it now, or have to deal with even more of it at a later time?

**The truth is that you can do it.**

And it won't be nearly as difficult as you might now imagine. The sooner you begin, the less there will be to surmount and the faster you will progress and move on with your life.

Why wait any longer?

You have the courage to be happy.

> *'All our dreams can come true,*
> *if we have the courage to pursue them'*
> **Walt Disney**

# A Sense of Joy

~

Just last weekend I was browsing in one of my favourite used bookshops and came across a slim volume that unexpectedly held a small pressed flower. The book was old, its pages yellowed by time, and the flower was dry and faded.

There was no way of knowing who had pressed that little flower between those pages, no inscription or distinguishing mark that might give a clue. It was simply there, resting patiently, a moment from someone's life, a memory, preserved and waiting.

Finding that small flower filled me with a warm feeling and a sense of joy.

It had been years since I last pressed a flower or a leaf between the pages of a book and, because flowers and books can so easily be lost to time, I had thought that it was now only the memory of these things that remained.

And then, slowly, it dawned on me that there is something more than the memory that remains and lives within me. After all, what has not been lost is the joy that came with those flowers; the joy that made me reach out and press those leaves.

**Everything that we have ever experienced is here inside us**. Time and the events of life can erase the circumstances and the surroundings, but it cannot remove the joy itself.

In truth, joy has no real need to be remembered. It is within us always and all we have to do is to recognise it, to allow it. It is there waiting as patiently as a flower pressed between the pages of a book.

Yes, the cover and the chapters will change, the colours will fade and the words will soften. But the joy itself is there within us, always fresh and new and waiting.

When we put joy into our lives and into the lives of others, it will always be there, and it will last far longer than even the prettiest of flowers.

Why not choose to do something today that will bring joy, something that will allow joy to blossom?

After all, the flowers that are pressed inside your heart can never fade.

*'It will never rain roses. When we want to have more roses,*
*we must plant more roses'*
**George Eliot**

# The Will to Grow

~

So many of the people who come to see me do so with the past weighing heavily on their shoulders and in their hearts.

Indeed, a big part of my job is to help them to see that whatever that past may have been, it is not and it never was them.

Each one of us has a past and, in one way or another, that past has conditioned us to behave in certain ways.

Inside all of us, mixed right in with the joy, there are negative habits, ancient angers and resentments, useless obsessions and worn out modes of being.

None of these things help us or anyone else. All of these things hinder our growth, stifling our own inner peace and lessening our humanity.

Because of this, we each have a constant need to let go and move on, to grow beyond the conditioning experiences and limiting confines of the past.

This takes courage, but more than this, for real change to take place we need to want to grow. We need to have the will to grow.

Indeed, this will to grow is perhaps the single most determining factor in the success or failure of therapy. Without this will to grow, little can really be accomplished.

**With this will to grow, wonderful and life changing things can and do happen.**

Yes, we may cherish the past and take wisdom from it. After all, it teaches us that life itself is a fleeting and a precious gift. But it is a gift that cannot be lived retrospectively. It can only be lived and appreciated moment by moment and it can only be lived in a forward direction.

There really is no need to wait any longer to truly live your gift.

The sooner you move on, the more wonderful your life will be. Yes, it will take some work, but not nearly as much work as carrying the past with you day in and day out.

All it takes is a genuine will to grow.

*'There came a time when the risk to remain tight in the bud was more painful than the risk it took to blossom'*
**Anais Nin**

# As the Days Shorten

~

December is here once more, and with it come the shorter winter days, the longer winter nights.

Indeed, in the Northern Hemisphere, December is the month with the shortest daylight hours of the year.

Yet even these shorter days can be a source of joy—if we allow it.

It really is all in the attitude.

Those of us who are early risers can choose to enjoy the peaceful, quiet pre-dawn moments and then watch as the transforming light discloses another fresh, brand new day.

**It is another wonderful opportunity to live and to be alive.**

Yet, if we look a little closer, we might find that this peace, this joy is not really there in the dawn itself—it is in our attitude, our response to the dawn. It is in our response to the opening of another opportunity, another invitation to live. It is inside us.

Inside each one of us there is peace and there is limitless joy. They are not there in some of us but absent in others.

No divine hand has allotted these things to a select chosen few while denying the rest of us.

No one has the option on joy or peace, any more than any one has the option on truth or love.

They are there inside each and every single one of us. In fact, they *are* each one of us. They are our very nature.

Awakening to this truth is awakening to life.

And the only reason that we are unaware of this is because we have been hypnotised to believe otherwise. We have bought into the fiction that we are our limiting beliefs, or that we are our past, or what that great therapist Gil Boyne called 'the greatest fiction of all' — that we are unlovable.

We have been deluded into believing that we are something less than we really are; something smaller than our wonderful, gifted self.

Yes, we can play small and choose to let the darkness frighten us, just as we can choose to be frightened by the light that is there, within each one of us.

We can do that. Or we can simply choose to let that light shine, remembering that just as there is a time to do, there is a time to be.

When we truly understand that the joy and the peace we seek is already here inside us, then we become free to live in and be guided by its light.

And in allowing our own light to shine, we automatically subconsciously encourage others to do the same.

We return to our birthright. We return to our self.

And when this happens, we live as we were intended to live — in peace and in joy. At last we see the light.

*'An age is called "dark," not because the light fails to shine*
*but because people refuse to see it'*
**James Michener**

# An Open Heart

~

I t won't be long now, here comes the festive season. Already the shops are milling with people busily buying gifts and treats in preparation for the end of year holidays.

For so many of us, this is a time of giving and of receiving; a time for open hands and open hearts.

As the year draws to its close, we treasure those special days when we come together with friends and loved ones. It is as if this season has granted us a special dispensation to give a little more of ourselves and to share the warmth and the pleasure of simply being alive.

In truth, of course, our lives are filled with special days: holidays, birthdays, anniversaries, and the most special day of all — today.

Today life itself begins all over again. Today life grants you a special dispensation; you have the chance to start afresh, to free yourself of the limiting beliefs and outmoded patterns and habits of the past.

Yes, today can be like so many other days that have already come and gone. But what is the point of endlessly repeating the past?

**You really do not need to wait for the calendar to tell you when to open your heart and begin to enjoy life**. Why not begin right now?

There really is no better time.

May you open your heart to joy, sharing the warmth with your world and with everyone in it this festive season.

*'If you keep a green bough in your heart,*
*then the singing bird will come'*
**Chinese Proverb**

# The Mountain and You

⁓

ust one more week and another year draws to its close. What kind of a year did you make it?

Whatever your life has been in this past year it has in some way changed you.

Whether it has been a marathon or a sprint, a stroll in the park or that mountain you have been climbing, you have moved, and it is through movement that we grow.

Though life itself is movement, sometimes we ourselves must slow down. We need to pace ourselves or we risk becoming stuck. But even this has its use. When we have been running too fast, or in the wrong direction, then feeling stuck can give us the space to draw breath and to reflect; it can provide that pause we need in order to take a different path up the mountain.

The sands of time will continue to run, but we ourselves must sometimes stop running. **No matter how busy and rushed we are, we can pause and take a little step back.** After all, a mountain is climbed one step at a time.

Yes, December is the end of a year, but it can also be the beginning of a newer, fresher you.

Take that step back, and the picture you'll see may not be of an ending, but of a brand new beginning.

No matter what is happening or not happening in your life right now, always remember that you have a choice. Mountain or no mountain, this coming year really can be your year.

Why wait any longer? Today is the day that you can finally choose to be you.

> *'It is not the mountain we conquer, but ourselves...'*
> **Edmund Hilary**

# The Gift

～

As we enter this final week of the year, with the gift-giving holiday season fully upon us, our eyes may already be focusing on the brand new year that's now only a matter of days away.

Isn't this the perfect time to glance back, to pause and reflect for a moment on the year that is almost over?

How did the past twelve months go for you? Did you wisely choose which bridges to cross and which to burn? Was it all smooth sailing, or did you encounter some stormy weather? Did you navigate through it, handling those unexpected twists and turns, those surprises that you just hadn't anticipated?

Well, in one way or another you must have done, because in one way or another you got through it all. Life may not have gone exactly as you'd planned, but you made it. From beginning to end, the ups and downs, the joys and the sadness, you came through and you're still here, living and alive.

Whatever your life has been this past year, you are wiser now, richer now because of it. Think now of that richness; think now of how fortunate you really are to be here. You may have spent your days working hard, striving for more and more, yet have you really paused to see how rich you already are?

**You are rich because you are alive. You are rich simply because life is yours.**

In this season of gift giving do not allow yourself to forget that you already have the greatest gift of all: You have life. Be grateful for this wonderful gift. The more you let yourself appreciate and value it, the better and more meaningful your life will be.

The gifts you give and receive this holiday season will lose their sparkle and fade. The life that you live will last and last if you live it with a sense of gratitude and love.

Happy holidays, dear reader, and may the New Year freshen, renew and light your way to your own special treasure, your own special sense of joy.

*'We can only be said to be alive in those moments*
*when our hearts are conscious of our treasures'*
**Thornton Wilder**

# Bring Peter Into Your Home!

∾

Want to benefit from Peter's wonderful therapeutic gift, but unable to visit him personally?

Now there is a solution.

Peter's unique state-of-the-art therapeutic hypnosis recordings are available in the form of instant Mp3 downloads or CDs, so that those who cannot visit him personally are able to benefit from aspects of his advanced hypnotherapy in the comfort of their own home.

No matter where you are in the world or in life, Peter's powerful instant hypnosis downloads and CDs can help bring real change into your life.

Why not begin your journey today?


Visit the website:
www.hypnosiscdmp3downloads.com

Also available on Amazon

www.ingramcontent.com/pod-product-compliance
Lightning Source LLC
Chambersburg PA
CBHW050531280326
41933CB00011B/1548